I0532212

A FLAWED MAN'S PLANS
IN GOD'S HANDS

LIVE A BETTER, FULLER LIFE WITH FEWER FLAWS AND MORE JOY!

DR. HARRY HOBBS WITH ERICA HOBBS

Adam Colwell's writeworks

A Flawed Man's Plans in God's Hands
by Dr. Harry Hobbs with Erica Hobbs
© 2023 by Dr. Harry Hobbs. All rights reserved.

Editing by Adam Colwell's WriteWorks, LLC, Adam Colwell and
Ginger Colwell
Cover and interior design by Clarity Designworks
Published by Adam Colwell's WriteWorks, LLC
Printed in the United States of America
ISBN (Paperback): 979-8-9864882-8-8
ISBN (eBook): 979-8-9864882-9-5

All Bible quotations are from THE HOLY BIBLE, NEW
INTERNATIONAL VERSION® Copyright© 1973, 1978, 1984,
2011 by Biblica, Inc.™ Used by permission of Zondervan.

Scripture marked AMP in the book endorsements is taken from
the AMPLIFIED® BIBLE, Copyright© 1954, 1958, 1962, 1964,
1965, 1987 by the Lockman Foundation. Used by Permission.
www.lockman.org

All rights reserved. Except in the case of brief quotations embodied
in critical articles and reviews, no portion of this book may be
reproduced, stored in a retrieval system, or transmitted in any form
or by any means—electronic, mechanical, photocopy, recording,
scanning, or other—without the prior written permission from the
author. None of the material in this book may be reproduced for any
commercial promotion, advertising or sale of a product or service.

While the author has made every effort to provide accurate internet
addresses at the time of publication, neither the publisher nor the
author assumes any responsibility for errors or for changes that occur
after publication. Further, the publisher does not have any control
over and does not assume any responsibility for author or third-party
websites or their content.

What they're saying about
A Flawed Man's Plans in God's Hands

In this book, Erica and Harry offer their real-life story in a way all readers can appreciate. It is about truth and being honest with yourself. It will help you accept your flaws and understand no one is perfect. For them to be so open and humble was refreshing, but it also demonstrated their willingness to sacrifice in order to help others. With each page filled with heartfelt messages, Scripture, and faith, it is clear the Hobbs family poured their heart and soul into this book.

For almost 10 years I have been a friend and partner in life to both Erica and Harry. They are great mentors and truly believe in the value of all people. They have made it their purpose to encourage others and be a positive influence on the people they meet and the world.

I highly encourage you to read this book and gain from their lessons learned. I will use their words and stories for self-encouragement, and I will also recommend this book to anyone wanting to know of God's joy and happiness.

Leon Wass
Manager, Energy Services, Huntsville Utilities,
Huntsville, Alabama

Radical honesty at its best, *A Flawed Man's Plans in God's Hands* is a captivating and suspenseful story of the human struggle and God's pursuit. My friend, Dr. Hobbs, and his wife, Erica, remind us that we are never outside God's reach. With arms open wide, God forgives, heals, restores, and refines. In the end, the narrative of God prevails. Whatever happens in life, God is faithful—no matter what.

This is a must-read book about the persistent and ever-present encounter between God and humankind. From the first page to the last, *A Flawed Man's Plans in God's Hands* will not disappoint.

Charles H. Lahmon
Chaplain (LTC), USA Garrison Chaplain, USAG Redstone
Arsenal, Huntsville, Alabama

In *A Flawed Man's Plans in God's Hands*, Harry Hobbs has shared his life story with us. I met Mr. Hobbs 22 years ago while we were both in the Army. Other than his formal military biography, I knew very little compared to what the book provided. Mr. Hobbs goes in depth regarding his childhood, his family, and the obstacles and challenges that he faced to become the Christian he is today. This book is a testament of his faith in God and the rewards for serving God.

In Chapter 5, Dr. Hobbs revealed a pivotal turning point in his life. It "galvanized" him as a person and challenged his desire to be a Christian. Finally, Dr. Hobbs leaves us with eight truths that helped him become a better leader. Excellent guidance for all. I highly recommend the book. His thoughts and reflections in the final chapter are a blueprint for a successful life. A must read.

Farrell Chiles
Retired Chief Warrant Officer Four and author of several books including three on African American Warrant Officers, one on female African American Warrant Officers, and *As BIG As It Gets—A Chairman of the Board's Rise and Tenure at the Top—Lessons In Leadership*.

This book is a definite addition to your collection of literature. It inspires and uplifts its readers in every sense to achieve excellent outcomes from challenges in life. The author shares candid episodes of end-of-the-road circumstances that flourished into victorious steps forward which accomplished new opportunities in his and his wife's life. The life lessons in this book will keep you enthused and capture your attention while leaving you starving for more. This book will undoubtedly enlighten you as you walk through a courageous journey to see success in your own life.

After reading this book, you will fully understand how God's plan will prevail in your life, no matter what you are facing.

Dr. Karockas "Doc Rock" Watkins
CEO/President/Executive Director, Ability Plus, Inc. and Vision Excellence Company, Huntsville, Alabama

Harry and Erica Hobbs are my lifelong friends. They are special people who have overcome every challenge they've encountered in life. They have served our nation as a military family and as volunteers in our great community. Harry has served in harm's way as a combat veteran. We owe so much to them and their wonderful family—and are grateful to them for sharing their story in this wonderful book.

Skip Vaughn
U.S. Army Garrison-Redstone public affairs specialist, newspaper journalist, and published author of *Vietnam Revisited*, published in 2017.

I first met Dr. Harry Hobbs while we were adjunct professors at Florida Tech. I remembered that Harry always wore a three-piece suit. What I did not know at that time was that Harry has also worn military and police uniform—suits that you will see in his story.

We all wear suits or uniforms to some degree. The question is, do we share what is underneath them, like Harry does in this engaging story, to help others. His is a story of love and growth with his early turbulent life, his bride, Erica, their family, his country, the military, and our gracious Lord. It is a deep and revealing journey that will engage the reader in the ever-present question of free will and life purpose. It is a tapestry of life that reveals God's presence and love in so many crucibles that we and others experience.

Harry's story reveals, as Proverbs 16:9 says, "A man's mind plans his way [as he journeys through life], But the Lord directs his steps and establishes them." (AMP)

Dr. J.D. Cerny
Nathan M. Bisk College of Business, Florida Tech University, Huntsville, Alabama.

A transformative experience, the authors' writing and insights will cause someone's personal setbacks and failures to be transformed by divine intervention through faith and prayers.

Dr. Earnest L. Davis
CEO/President, North Alabama Center for Educational Excellence, Huntsville, Alabama

CONTENTS

To our children and our grandchildren. We love you all and we pray all of your questions about your father/mother and Papa/Lola have been revealed to you in this book in a way so you can better understand, love, and forgive us, in spite of our many flaws.

To my wife, Erica, for helping me write this book, and for her unwavering support and encouragement for over 42 years. She has literally been the wind beneath my wings since we met. My wife has provided me with unbelievable emotional and spiritual support through the many years of my mistakes and missteps. I would not have completed this work or reached any level of success in life without Erica by my side. I love you, Erica Hobbs, and I thank you for being my wife and my best friend. Thank you for looking past my shortcomings and sins to see the Christian man I could become.

To anyone who may think they cannot overcome their shortcomings, sins, and flaws—know that it is possible through faith, hard work, dedication, and a great support team. No one is an island. It takes a village to overcome failures in life. For those who are in the middle of overcoming their flaws and shortcomings, may God bless you with a village that will support you as you transform your life into what God would have you to be.

ACKNOWLEDGEMENTS

First, we want to acknowledge our Lord and Savior, Jesus Christ, for giving us the strength, courage, and knowledge to complete this arduous journey of self-reflection and growth.

I want to acknowledge and thank Mr. Adam Colwell for his guidance and leadership throughout this process. Adam is our editor, friend, motivator, and brother in Christ. His guidance and mentorship were instrumental to the direction we took for our book.

I also want to thank our friend and brother in Christ, Dr. Karockas Watkins, for his urging to write our book and for introducing us to Adam. Karockas inspired us to reveal our true story and allow others to learn from our mistakes and flaws.

This book could not have been written without our brother-in-law, Bill Steele, and Erica's childhood friend, Shanna. Thank you, Bill, for always supporting us and always being available to help mentor me throughout my young adulthood and military career. I also want to thank you for allowing us to visit your office that day in early February 1981. You have always been my role model and big brother. Thank you to Erica's friend in high school for telling me that Erica really did like me even though she didn't show it during our conversation that night at the disco.

I also want to thank my brother who is two years older than me, Hugh, for helping Erica get all of her paperwork and identification cards in order, so she could fly to Germany when she graduated high school. Thank you, brother, for being there with me in Germany when our first daughter was born. I know God is real just from being a witness to your Christian transformation. I also know that love can overcome a multitude of sins and heal old wounds.

We also want to thank our pastor and mentors from the International Church of God of Prophecy in Germany. We attended the International Church of God of Prophecy during two of our four tours of duty in Germany. Thank you to Pastor Endecott and his wife, Wanda, and to church members Stephan Reinhold, and his wife, Brenda. Their spiritual guidance, patience, and prayers helped us to work on, and eventually overcome, our poor parenting skills.

We also want to thank our Christian mentors for the last two decades, Tom and Ann Albertson and Rich and Sue Goldsmith, for your encouragement, guidance and Christian example you have set through the years.

We want to thank our families that raised us. We both know they did all they could to provide us with a Christian foundation for success in life. God never fails and always forgives through His Son, Jesus.

FOREWORD

By Lt. Colonel Alexander W. Steele
United States Army Reserves (Retired)

Dr. Harry Hobbs takes us on a journey from his childhood to his young adulthood when he and Erica meet, then through demanding, but greatly rewarding, military and civilian careers. The book combines both of their journeys from dating, to marriage and children, and all the joys and challenges of marriage and family life that are coupled with the joys and challenges of life overall that they experienced together.

The content of this book consists of heartfelt, engaging, and truthful, real-life events. Harry recounts many of his experiences as a biracial and impoverished child growing up in Kentucky during the 1960s and 1970s who faced numerous societal obstacles as well as periodic discriminatory treatment from family members—and whose single mother suffered from mental illness which frequently caused her to be institutionalized. He inspires us with his successes and very earnestly discusses his shortcomings.

Harry takes us through his military career as he achieves and traverses the ranks and numerous duty assignments spanning nearly 30 years. We see Harry as a young private suffering burns when a heating unit exploded in his face after he had been ordered to ignite the apparatus by a careless officer. We grow with him as he rapidly ascends the Army ranks, and we walk side-by-side with him in throughout his combat experiences in Operation Desert Storm and Operation Joint Endeavor.

As Harry recounts his military and civilian careers, we are given insight into how challenges and sacrifices are the requisites of professional growth and success. Additionally, we are candidly shown the positive, as well as the negative, aspects of such.

During the many years that I have known Harry and Erica, I have seen them grow from young adults to newlyweds beginning and establishing their foothold in following Christ. I have been able to recognize and admire them as people who walk the walk just like they talk the talk! I first met Erica when she was a young child because I began dating her sister in 1972 shortly after I returned from a tour of duty in Vietnam. After her sister and I married, I was able to watch Erica grow, and over the years become the kind, loving, and spiritually strong woman that she is today.

Although this book is reflective of many of Harry's experiences, it was developed with the combined effort and consensus of him and his wife. It is an honest account of their experiences, written for the purpose of sharing their journey, that will hopefully serve as encouragement and reinforcement for you to seek the Lord. Throughout the course of the entire book, biblical scriptures are blended in and used to reflect upon their lived experiences, and they serve as testimony as well as encouragement for you to study the Word of God.

The essence of this book is truly an open door which provides the opportunity for you to learn from the experiences of others and to develop and enhance your own Christian faith.

AUTHOR'S NOTE

This is my story, along with my wife, Erica's, observations. My perceptions or viewpoints of the events and circumstances in this book may differ from my siblings, family members, and others because this represents my memory of my experiences. Therefore, my wife and I have chosen to omit most proper names of those who have been a part of our story, including family members. We want to respect their anonymity. There are certain stories that we have not shared because family or friends have requested that we not do so due to personal reasons and concerns. We have respected those requests even though we believe that some of those stories, if shared, would have shown even more how great God really is and that He still reigns today!

Matching memory to reality is always difficult. I respect that family, friends, or others may disagree with my story and the way I wrote it, and I intend no offense to anyone. I love my family dearly, and I thank God that my mother birthed me and that my aunt and grandmother raised me. I pray that anyone who I have offended through my youthful sins of commission or omission will find it in their hearts to forgive me, just as I have had to forgive others for the things they have done against me. My plea is especially fervent to those who will not forgive others but profess to be Christians. How can we lead others to Jesus when we do not forgive the flaws of others knowing we have flaws ourselves?

My sole focus in *A Flawed Man's Plans in God's Hands* is to demonstrate that God is real and to help people overcome obstacles in order to be all they can be in life! Erica and I will share stories of our childhoods, how we met and fell in love, life in the United States Army, and our challenges in raising children, confronting racism and prejudice, finding our faith in Christ, succeeding in corporate America, and overcoming our human weaknesses and failures in order to help others. We will pepper in Bible verses, and teachings from them, throughout my story to further showcase God's glory, forgiveness, strength, and guidance as they were manifested in our lives. We will also share lessons learned for those who may find themselves in situations similar to ours.

I am often called upon to speak at seminars, graduations, business conferences, youth groups, civic organizations, and every level of the education system to declare how I became so successful. Others have told me that they think I must be perfect to have pulled myself up by my bootstraps to overcome poverty, abandonment, racism, and medical challenges to become an executive at a highly successful organization. The truth, of course, is that I am far from perfect—and I use *A Flawed Man's Plans in God's Hands* to openly reveal just some of my failings because it is time to bring my shortcomings into the light. Why? There is no success without pain. Pain brings forth growth, resolve, maturity, and appreciation for life. I don't want people to see a snapshot of my success without seeing the pain and struggle it took to get here.

While some readers may think less of me for revealing my failings, I am convinced others will see me in a more positive light because I have been so transparent to showcase my flaws so that others can learn from my mistakes. No one is perfect. We all make mistakes, and God knows I made my fair share and then some—yet in John 8:7, Jesus told the sinful woman's accusers, "Let any one of you who is without sin be the first to throw a stone at her."

I am still overcoming obstacles in my life, but I know, even as a flawed man, that if I keep my plan in God's hands, I will overcome! I am encouraged by Psalm 27:1-2. "The Lord is my light and salvation—whom shall I fear? The Lord is the stronghold of my life—of whom shall I be afraid? When the wicked advance against me to devour me, it is my enemies and my foes who will stumble and fall."

OBSTACLES TO THE PLAN

I've certainly dealt with a lion's share of obstacles in pursuit of a better, fuller life with fewer flaws and more joy—but three in particular were pivotal and served to set the stage for my entire story.

The first obstacle could've prevented me from being here at all.

I was born out of wedlock, the child of a white father and a black mother, on July 7, 1960, in Louisville, Kentucky. To say the least, it was quite taboo for a white and a black to be a couple south of the Mason-Dixon line, but the racial situation was just the beginning of my troubles. I have only rumors to inform who my father was and what he did for a living. They say his name was John and that he was a police officer, but he was never involved in my life, and I never met him. He passed away some time ago. My mother was 29 when I came along, but she had been diagnosed with bipolar manic depression and was hospitalized at a mental health facility for about 90 percent of my upbringing.

How the two of them came together, I do not know, but when it was discovered that my momma was pregnant with me, she was deemed incapable of making the decision to keep me or not. It's understandable. She was a mentally ill black woman in and out of a mental health facility who already had five children and was separated from her husband, living in poverty, and made pregnant by a white man. So, though it was not at all an accepted part of black culture, would have been very hard to obtain, and certainly would have been unsafe as well as illegal, an abortion was a very real possibility.

It was my grandmother and my aunt who ultimately saved my life, and after I was born, decided to keep me instead of putting me up for adoption. My momma came out of the mental health facility to give birth to me, and she went right back in afterward.

My aunt was a staunch United Methodist, and I believe it was because she was a woman of faith that I wasn't aborted and that she and her family took me in.

By all rights, I shouldn't be here. Yet because of the intervention of my extended family, I am. It was the first thread of the tapestry of God's presence working in my life.

But that didn't mean it was going to be easy. There were as many as 15 of us at a time living in the same shotgun-style house at 3514 Ethel Avenue off of Old Shepherdsville Road in a very rural area outside of Louisville. The narrow abode was no more than 12 feet wide with rooms arranged one behind the other and doors at each end of the house.

We had no running water or electricity. We had to use the bathroom in a rickety, smelly outhouse and bathe in a long, rectangular metal tub with handles at each end in case it needed to be carried somewhere. The water went almost as deep as a wading pool, and we took turns on bath night, which meant not everyone got clean water.

The tub was in a wooden shed located nearly 30 yards behind the house that my grandfather and some other family members had built. I remember that shed well, in that it was one of the only places where any of us could enjoy any privacy. It was sturdy, with four cinder block steps leading up to the entrance, and it was sizable, as large as a full-size living room. It had wooden beams with items stored in the rafters, glass windows, and a lock on the door that certainly came in handy when we were bathing. Kerosene lamps and candles served as lighting. The shed contained everything from my grandfather's carpentry tools and my grandmother's foot-operated sewing machine to old clothes and toys.

Two wood and coal burning stoves were all we had in the house to heat our bathing and cooking water, and everyone could be sitting at the dinner table each night. There were my five older siblings (two sisters and three brothers), four of my cousins, and five adults: Big Mama, Big Daddy, my aunt and uncle, and my mother whenever she was visiting from the mental health facility. I usually sat to the left of my grandmother at the head of the table. We never went hungry, though there was no chance of anyone becoming overweight, either. Our resources were limited, but my grandmother was an excellent resource manager. Meatloaf and fried chicken were common meals and my favorites. We had chickens on the property. It was not unusual for me to be playing with a chicken one day and eating it the next.

We were downwind of a pig farm where the animals were kept until they were slaughtered. The stench permeated the atmosphere of our home, getting in our clothes and taking up residence in our noses. To say we lived in abject poverty was putting it kindly. We scraped by on meager funding and assistance from the government, and my grandparents worked hard at their day jobs to support us. My grandmother cleaned homes. My grandfather had a landscaping business.

My earliest childhood memories include going to visit my momma every couple of months at the mental health facility. I can still remember the smell of the hallways, a nauseating cocktail of bleach, urine, and feces, and seeing the other patients roaming the halls and displaying the characteristics you'd imagine from individuals in that type of environment. It was pretty traumatic for a six-year-old boy. One visit was particularly significant. It was a sunny, spring day, so we were able to sit outside at a picnic table in the courtyard. The atmosphere there was much better than in the common area where visitors met with patients most of the time. Momma was nicely dressed, in good spirits, and noticeably more coherent than usual. That was likely because she hadn't recently undergone electroshock therapy or wasn't hopped up on psychiatric drugs.

As we sat across from each other, my momma's eyes met mine. She was as present as I'd ever seen her.

"You are smart," she said, smiling. "I know in my heart that you will become someone important one day."

That was one of the few times my momma spoke into my life when I was little, and it stayed with me, not so much for what was said, but because of who said it. In the years ahead, I'd begin to believe that maybe my momma was right. I could do something more than most people born into my unfortunate circumstances. Perhaps there would even be some type of miracle that God would provide to allow me to make that happen.

At home, there were times that I felt traumatized due to the way I was sometimes treated by members of my family. I wasn't the only one in my home who received physical or verbal mistreatment, but I was regularly the recipient of aggressive behavior directed at me solely because I was so physically different from everyone else. One of the reasons I sat so close to my grandmother at the dinner table was so she could ensure I got a reprieve from the overly harsh physical and verbal behavior directed toward me by several family members—primarily my siblings.

Yet there's no doubt in my mind that my family handled me and the other children as best they could when you consider the nation's situation at the time and our own economic challenges. Any parent or guardian feels they could have done things better, and I thank God that I didn't have to take on the challenges and responsibilities faced by my aunt, Big Mama, and Big Daddy. I don't believe anyone in our family could have done any better, considering the circumstances.

I tried my best to not do anything that would disappoint my grandparents—especially my grandmother, Big Mama. A strict authoritarian, she believed in a liberal amount of corporal punishment delivered with little to no notice. In her mind, she was helping us stay on the right path in life. She didn't mean it to be as harsh as it appeared. In her heart, she believed that discipline was the route to success as people of color in a very strict, white-dominated world. She grew up in the Depression years and was only a couple of generations removed from slavery. So, there was no left or right with her. We did what she told us to do, or we were going to get it.

If she'd wanted, Big Mama could have just as easily put me and my siblings in foster care or made us wards of the state, yet she took us in and tried to do the best she could to raise us. Her approach to discipline was what it was, but only God knows how bad it could have been if she had not stepped up to take us all in when she didn't have to. I have heard rumblings over the years from some family members who have said she did it for the money the state gave her, but there was no amount of money that would have been enough to compensate for what she had to experience dealing with us at her advanced age and with such minimal resources.

I loved Big Mama. She is a hero to me. Starting when I was eight years of age, I always got to stay home alone with her on Friday nights when one of my cousins, a great football player who'd later be drafted into the National Football League, had game nights at his high school. I didn't like to attend the games because of the way I negatively stood out among the mostly black fans in attendance. I also knew those nights were the only individual time I could have with my grandmother.

Big Mama was less stressed out and very kind to me on those nights. She was more relaxed and loving. She spoke kinder and walked softer. Even then, I understood that she had been through many crucibles in her life, and I somehow wanted to make her life better, not worse. We spent most of our time together talking, and I was at that age when I was starting to ask questions, most of them revolving around the theme of, "Why am I so different?" I was beginning to become self-aware, and she responded to my queries as best she could.

I can still feel her pat my head and rub my hair as she served special snacks like orange slices (the chewy candy kind with a sugar coating) and chocolate drops. If everyone was still out late and it was time for bed, she let me get in bed and fall asleep with her until they got home. It was nice to fall asleep near Big Mama. I also adored my grandfather, Big Daddy. I was very close to him, and later, after we moved into a new house in 1971, we often watched old cowboy movies and football games together.

With their shared influence in my life, it was no wonder, then, I was able to daydream of someday seeking a better life. It usually happened whenever the train came rumbling down the tracks on the backside of our property about 100 feet away from the home. As the *clackety-clack* of the passing cars shook the house to its foundations, I'd sit in the kitchen, peer out the window at the train, and wish for the day when I could ride away, see the world, and never again have to live poor and destitute.

———

The second obstacle, or set of barriers, that I had to overcome involved a literal baptism by fire.

It began when I was seven years old. My momma was visiting from the mental health facility. We were talking in one of the bedrooms when I became obstinate and started trying to back away from her down the hallway. Without me noticing, my older brother had come into the house behind me carrying a big pot of boiling water for cooking.

> I was able to daydream of someday seeking a better life.

Biff! We collided with each other accidentally as he was coming around the corner—and the searing water sloshed over the rim of the pot and splashed onto my hips and lower back. I screamed as my aunt and another family member ripped my shirt and pants off because the clothes had started to adhere to my skin from the heat.

Blistered and bloody, I had third degree burns from the scalding water.

The whole thing was my fault. I wasn't used to spending time with my momma, and I simply didn't want to do what she said. In the moment, I was probably a little frightened of her, but I certainly do not blame her for what happened. At any rate, Big Mama was away working during the day, and my aunt happened to be staying with us at the time, so she was the one who ended up taking care of me in the days that followed. My aunt held me at night, rocking me, humming a little tune, and telling me I was going to be alright. The burns hurt so bad as layers of my skin peeled off, but she always managed to comfort me. That was her role in our family. If Big Mama was the heavy for me and the rest of the kids, my aunt was the other side of that. In fact, she was the closest thing I had to a real mother aside from Big Mama.

I was pulled out of school for a while and sent to a burn specialist. I don't know how my family managed to do that considering what little we had, but they did. Over a period of several weeks, every scab had to be slowly and painfully removed to prevent scarring.

It was horrible, and only the first of my encounters with burning heat. Two years later, I managed to rub against the big wood and coal burning stove in the center of the home near my grandmother's bedroom. The outside of the stove was always hot, and with so many people in our house and the area being so tight, it was hard to avoid.

I was likely playing. No one had purposefully pushed me or tried to harm me. It was just another accident, completely inadvertent—but it was almost as harmful as before. I got a second degree burn on the back of my right hand. I was still able to make a fist and move my fingers, but it sure hurt to do so. Again, my skin blistered and bled, and it gradually peeled off over the next two weeks, but this time I didn't have to see a doctor. Yet even then, at age nine, I couldn't help but wonder if this was now becoming a pattern. *Am I going to keep getting burned?*

Just one year later, my two brothers and I had moved from my grandmother's home into a house with my momma and her boyfriend. My other siblings were grown and on their own. Momma had been doing well enough to be released from the mental health facility, find work, and stay in her own place, an older home near downtown Louisville. I was so very proud of her. For the first time in my life, she was conducting herself like a responsible adult and taking care of her children. I didn't know how long it would last, but it was like paradise to me because I could do simple things like give her a hug whenever I wanted to. I came home from school one afternoon to find that she had purchased some new bedding for me. I thought it was as cool as a trip to Disney World, and I gave her the biggest hug! My momma seemed stable and happy, and I couldn't help but hope, *Maybe we are becoming just like a normal family.*

Another thing that made the new bedding that much more significant was that I had my own room. At Big Mama's, I shared a bedroom with my two brothers. I suppose my room at momma's wasn't anything to brag about. It was small and basic with a bed, a chair, a desk, and a lamp. It had a window, and since it was on the second floor, it gave me a bird's eye view of the neighborhood park with its fading grass, overgrown trees, and old swing set and slide. But I truly loved it. I didn't have a bookshelf, so I kept my beloved Brains Benton and Hardy Boys mystery books between bookends on my desk, my comics stacked beside them. Having my own room made me feel important, validated, cared for, and valued. It's not that I wasn't all of those when I was with Big Mama and the extended family, but I felt more independent. I could be by myself. I was an individual.

One more positive aspect of living with my momma was the school I attended: Booker T. Washington Elementary. It was an all-black school, so I was the only half-white/half-black child on campus. The principal assigned teachers to keep watch over me all day to ensure I would be safe from being attacked by the black kids because of my appearance. I may have looked like the enemy to them, and they tried to take out their frustrations on me by threatening to beat me up in the hallways. But I learned a lot about how to collaborate, negotiate, and get along with others, and I was able to talk my way out of those potential fights. Looking back now, I know my time at Booker T. Washington was an important building block for my greater journey.

All was truly well living with momma—but fire was about to intervene again in my life in an even more devastating way.

Early one evening, about seven o'clock at night, I was in the living room when we heard a neighbor outside yelling that we needed to get out of the house right away. I didn't smell or see anything indicating something was wrong, but I knew I had better listen to an adult who was clearly trying to help us.

Ironically, on my way outside, I grabbed one of my most treasured toys: a red, metal fire engine. It had all the bells and whistles: a light-up siren with battery-operated lights, a beautifully painted and detailed chassis, a white folding ladder attached to a crane on the back of the engine, and real rubber wheels with chrome hubcaps. I had recently received it as a birthday gift, and I loved playing with it in the living room while watching cartoons every afternoon. As I made my escape, somehow my mind convinced me, *You are not leaving your fire engine behind.*

Next thing I remember, I was sitting on the sidewalk across from the house as it burned to the ground. I later learned a gas leak caused the blaze. The homes were so old and built so closely together. I gazed across at the flames and charred walls, down at my little fire engine, then up at the actual firemen and trucks putting out the fire. It was absolutely surreal.

A man and a woman from The Salvation Army then drove up, looking all official in their black jackets trimmed in red. They appeared to be so professional and kind. The gentleman came up to me to ask if I was okay before handing me a small box of animal crackers. I opened the box, grabbed a lion, my favorite animal, and popped it into my mouth. *Wow,* I thought. *These are really good people trying to help.* That planted a seed within me to help other people in need that would sprout later in my life.

The man and woman marshalled their resources, including providing someplace for us to stay that night. We were glad we were alive, but everyone was crying, and my momma was beside herself. In the days that followed, it quickly became clear to me that the short time I'd had living with my momma was not going to last. Two weeks later, my brothers and I were back with Big Mama, and my momma was back in the mental health facility. I can only imagine what that tragedy took from her. She had been given a chance to make life work, but the loss was simply too great for her mentally.

As for me, I was not burned or otherwise injured by the fire, but it was just another setback from the same source. It seemed I simply couldn't get away from it.

By 1978, I had enlisted in the United States Army. Young, fit, and with all the potential to succeed, I was also headstrong, foolish, and not making the best decisions. I knew I really wasn't being the soldier—and person—I could be. After basic training was completed, I would serve my first tour of duty at Ft. Knox. Located just south of Louisville, Ft. Knox allowed me to still be near home and family. During this time, it also allowed me to hang out with my high school friends on the weekends, smoking dope, drinking, being sexually promiscuous, and essentially doing things that were not conducive to being a soldier.

One such weekend, I was at the Kentucky State Fair with my nine-year-old nephew and one of my buddies from high school. Sitting in the parking lot, I had an open six-pack of beer and some marijuana in the car, and one of the police officers who was patrolling the lot saw us.

"Hey, there!" he said as he approached. "I need all of you to get out of the car."

My heart raced while I did as he said. He motioned toward me. "Let me see your I.D."

He took a look at it, then at me. "You're a soldier, and you are probably trying to change your life."

It wasn't a question, but I nodded in meek agreement anyway.

"Guess what?" he continued. "I'm gonna allow you to change your life today and take one more step in the right direction. I'm going to take this six-pack and the marijuana, and then I'm going to let you go. I don't want you to ever forget the chance I just gave you to be a better person."

I hadn't realized I was holding my breath, and I let out a deep sigh of relief. He could have easily run me downtown. I was 19 years old, and I had my nephew, a minor, with me in the vehicle. I *should've* gotten in trouble—and if I had been cited, I could have lost rank or been processed out of the Army altogether, losing money, and more importantly, my good standing as a soldier. Although I wasn't living my life then as a Christian, I had been raised to do so. For some reason, I sensed that God was looking out for me, even if I didn't yet know why. It wasn't that I was being a bad person or hurting anyone, but I knew in my heart that I was not living up to my potential. I was just going through the motions, doing the bare minimum as a soldier and in life in general.

I knew in my heart that I was not living up to my potential.

I had been in the Army for a couple of years when, in January 1980, I was sent on a winter military training exercise at Ft. Drum, New York. By then, I had renewed a relationship with a young lady I had dated while in high school, and we had agreed to get married.

The morning of January 15, I was ordered by my lieutenant to light the Yukon stove we were using to heat our chilly tent during the exercise. The tent was attached to the track vehicle immediately behind our armored personnel carrier. Five other soldiers were sitting in folding chairs around the stove, a dark grey, rectangular metal box with front legs like an old potbelly and an exhaust pipe leading up to the ceiling of the tent. While it was only supposed to be used for heating the space, it wasn't unusual for fellow soldiers to sit their canteens on it to heat water for coffee. The opening of the stove was directly in the front.

I didn't find out until later how many times that Yukon stove had become combustible, and that it had a history of leaking gas and exploding upon being lit. But I already sensed it was dangerous because I'd seen a bit of a flash burst forth from the opening when others had lighted it previously.

I informed my lieutenant that I was not trained on the stove and that I had been burned before. "I'm very nervous around gas and fires," I admitted.

He was unmoved. He instructed me to light a match and throw it in the stove, adding that the stove was already primed. "Private," he commanded, "do what I told you to do. Light the fire."

Sssffff. I struck the match, bent down about a foot away from the front of the Yukon, and tossed the tiny flame into the opening.

Whoosh. A fireball of hot force and energy billowed out and over my face.

The sweet, acrid scent of natural gas flooded my nostrils. My eyes and mouth instinctively snapped shut, but I saw a split second of flame before it hit me.

My entire face and neck were burned. My eyebrows were singed away. The only thing that saved the hair on my head was my olive drab cold weather cap. Similar to Russian flap hats, it's thick fur and hide protected my scalp and ears, but that was all it shielded.

My scorched skin sizzled and smelled like overly burned bacon.

I instantly went into shock, but that didn't prevent me from hearing my fellow soldiers screaming and hollering as I lay there burning until someone put a towel over my face to snuff out the flames.

"Oh, my God! It looks bad!" one person yelled out.

"He's going to be scarred for life!" another bellowed.

Their cries only made it worse. Because the nerve endings on my head had been cauterized, I couldn't feel anything. *Really? Is it that bad?* I absurdly thought. Those questions were cruelly answered moments later when the pain kicked in.

The Yukon had a damaged fuel regulator and had been leaking gas all night into the bottom of the stove.

It all happened so quickly.

As I was medically evacuated to the burn unit at Ft. Drum, I silently muttered a prayer through the stabbing pain.

I hope my face isn't so damaged that my fiancé will want to leave me.

By the time I whipped up the courage to call her in Louisville two days later, I had received extensive treatment in the burn unit, including IV's and several cleanings and wraps. I'd waited that long to contact her not just because I was in and out of consciousness, but also so I'd know for sure how bad the burns were and what the diagnosis was—and it was bleak. I was informed that I was going to have to undergo repeated grafts, taking skin from other parts of my body and transferring it on to my face, due to the severity of my burns.

As I look back on that moment, I recall 1 Peter 1:6. It teaches, "In all this you greatly rejoice, though now for a little while you may have had to suffer grief in all kinds of trials. These have come so that the proven genuineness of your faith—of greater worth than gold, which perishes even though refined by fire—may result in praise, glory and honor when Jesus Christ is revealed." I had been through so much, and I had not yet returned to the faith of my youth. But I can see now how God was still working, through my injuries and through the relationship challenges about to unfold, so that the authenticity of my belief in the Lord could be brought forth. Even then, God was using trials to set the stage for my return to Him so that I may bring glory to Him today.

My fiancé listened quietly as I spoke to her, saying little, but I could tell, just from the sound of her voice, that our marriage wasn't going to happen. There was no strength, no encouragement, no love in her tone. Only cold acceptance, and a hint of resignation that I rightly interpreted as the beginning of the end.

I don't blame her today. It was clear that she simply wasn't going to be on board for everything that needed to be done for me to recover. It was too much. In the few conversations that followed that first call, I sensed that she didn't want to be the one to call it, but her heart wasn't in the relationship any longer, and neither was mine. I told her that I didn't expect her to put up with it, and she agreed.

A week into my initial treatments, I received some heartening news. One of the doctors said it was possible that I may not need skin grafts after all. They began using an advanced method of burned skin recovery that could heal my wounds over time without the aggressiveness of the grafts. It involved placing a new salve solution on the burns and then wrapping my face with gauze. The gauze would have to stay on for a number of days before the wraps were removed to allow my face to air dry and scab up, after which they would meticulously remove the scabs and repeat the process all over again. I looked like a mummy from the neck up while the gauze did its work, but it was much less invasive than skin grafts.

Even then, I was told it was going to take six months to a year before I'd really start to recover, and there was no way to tell just how much my face was going to look the way it had before. It was also likely that I would need plastic surgery to fully restore my facial skin and structure.

I deployed back to Ft. Knox with my unit about three weeks after I was burned. I finally went to my fiancé's home a month later, and she willingly gave back the high school ring that I had given to her as a placeholder for the wedding ring that I was saving up to buy for her. Again, we didn't say much to one another. Everything was understood, and I felt nothing but kindness toward her. I still do. I wouldn't expect anyone that young to make the commitment my injury required. It was a lot to process. I forgave her.

God knew she was not the wife for me—and later, the very ring she returned to me would help me win the heart of the woman I was destined to marry.

An investigation of the incident with the Yukon stove was completed by the time I got back to Ft. Knox. The lieutenant who had ordered me to light the stove was found to be in negligence of his duty due to his incompetence and the unsafe command he had issued to me. He was later relieved of his duties. I never forgot that leadership lesson and told myself that I would be a better leader in the Army if I was ever given the chance to do so.

Fire that had first blistered my body and my psyche when I was seven and nine, and the blaze that took away a brief childhood home and forever scarred my mother, had struck once more as an adult. This one, instant and incendiary, had almost cost me even more. Big Mama and Big Daddy, who had been informed of the accident shortly after it happened, were incredibly supportive of me as I went through my recovery. I was placed on light duty at Ft. Knox while I finished recovering from my burns, and my barracks roommate made sure I changed my bandages on time. The new burn recovery techniques worked, allowing my face to slowly heal, but it was very painful and embarrassing, especially when I stopped wearing bandages and had to keep my face uncovered.

About three months into the treatments, I was walking down the sidewalk at the local military Post Exchange store at Ft. Knox. It was a beautiful spring Saturday afternoon, and I had just finished buying some shoeshine polish for my boots. A young, blonde-haired woman in her thirties wearing a flowered dress was walking toward me on the other side of the sidewalk with a little boy, obviously her son, sporting a blue baseball cap, matching shirt, and denim shorts. As I watched them approach, I thought, *I hope that little boy never has to go through what I have.* I also mused, *I never had a chance to walk with my mom like that and hold her hand.*

As they passed, I saw the boy's smiling face turn to a befuddled frown as he looked directly at me.

I then heard him ask his mother a question.

"What is wrong with his face?"

It was a valid enough query. I still had to have scabs scraped off my forehead, cheeks, and jaw and plucked away from my eyebrows where they had nested after coming off my eyelids. New layers of skin grew in as each scab was removed. I probably looked like the Phantom of the Opera.

Yet the sense of embarrassment washed over me, making me want to scream, run away, hide, and cry. Self-pity and denial weighed down my mind in equal parts.

This is my lot in life. Why are all the cards stacked against me?

It was as if I was that scorched little child all over again.

I have never forgotten that feeling, and it compels me to constantly strive to remind people to be kind and forgiving to others because they never know what might happen to themselves or someone else in a flash of a moment. Years later, that memory would also steel my resolve and make me resilient. *If I can overcome that,* I recalled, *what else can I overcome?* Those burn incidents ultimately pushed me out of my comfort zone to seek higher learning, search for spiritual insight, take off my blinders, and become a better person. They also helped turn me into a servant leader.

But at the moment, I was wounded body, soul, and spirit, and it wasn't going to get any better. As the weeks of ongoing treatments turned to months, I went downhill mentally and emotionally. I began to think that I would never lead the life I could have led or marry the woman I should have married. I sank into a highly depressed state that I poorly chose to treat with drugs, alcohol, and promiscuity. My actions intensified in the wake of the accident at Ft. Drum, and they simply mirrored how I felt about myself.

They were easy, too. There was always someone in my military unit who sold marijuana, and I started to buy small doses to smoke on the weekends. My drink of choice was a rum and coke, and for a brief period of time, I became a private, habitual drinker. Most weekends, I was high and drunk at the same time. That led to more bad decision making. I'd hook up with a different girl every week. Their names or the details of their lives were unknown to me, and to this day, I'm ashamed of what I did with them. Hurting people migrate to hurting people, and those girls and I were nothing more than hurting people trying to make each other feel wanted for a moment.

> Hurting people migrate to hurting people.

Therefore, the last obstacle that I had to overcome—myself—led to the two greatest decisions of my life.

Despite the horrific burns I suffered that day at Ft. Drum, I was still taking for granted the ability to have an income, to be educated, and to be housed and fed by the Army. I wasn't exactly leading a stellar lifestyle, either. I was intent on going out and having a good time whenever I could. One weekend in May 1980, I went to a disco just outside one of the gates to Ft. Knox. I thought I was all that driving my little candy apple red Chevy Camaro Z-28 and blasting my Pioneer radio. I was rolling with one of my Army buddies, and like we used to say, it was a Friday night, we just got paid, and we were ready to get laid.

As we were sitting near the entrance of the club drinking our rum and cokes and listening to the music, K.C. and the Sunshine Band started singing, "That's The Way (I Like It)." Suddenly, three men burst in and went huffin', puffin', and blowin' up to the bar. It was obvious they were a little more than angry about something.

"Where is he at?" the larger of the men, a big, muscular Samoan, yelled. "I didn't get my full dime!"

Right away, I discerned that the trio was looking to hurt someone due to a drug deal gone wrong. The Samoan was prepared to do damage, too.

He had a machete in his hand.

Seeing and hearing what was happening, patrons began running left and right to flee the scene, and perhaps I should've, too—but something rose up within me that I didn't expect. It may have been the Eagle Scout in me from my five years of membership as a teen: loyal, helpful, and brave. Maybe it was the hand-to-hand combat training I had received or the past Kung Fu classes I had taken and recently resumed since my burn injury. Or it could have simply been the rum and cokes had gone to my head.

Whatever it was, I leaped from my seat, sprinted across the dance floor, and went after the beefy Polynesian with the enormous knife.

K.C.'s lyrics provided an interesting backdrop for what followed.

"When you take me by the hand..."

Boom! I sidestepped the Samoan and gave him a hip throw onto the floor.

"Tell me I'm you lovin' man..."

Clang! I heard the machete hit the concrete and slide away from the big man.

"When you give me all your love…"

Whack! On top of him, I leaned my full force into him with a knee to his chest.

"And do it babe the very best you can!"

Ooof! As I subdued my opponent, I exulted as others jumped in to take out the other two men.

"That's the way, aha, aha, I like it, aha, aha!"

In no time, I heard the police sirens arriving from the station just down the road from the disco.

I was just trying to do the right thing—aha, aha—and it worked out brilliantly.

As though it was planned that way, Carl Douglas' "Kung Fu Fighting" began pumping through the speakers, and I returned to my table. Moments later, as the police cleared out the riffraff, the disco owner, a tall, multi-racial man wearing a shiny silk shirt with a giant collar, came up to me. His smile couldn't hide his sense of surprise at what he'd just seen me do.

"How would you like to be my bouncer?" He paused. "Extra money. Meet girls."

It seemed only yesterday that a stove had blown up in my face.

What do I have to lose?

I took the gig. It made me feel important. Here he was trusting me, a 19-year-old, with security. Full of vim and vigor, I took on the bouncer role like some Brooklyn tough guy from *Saturday Night Fever*.

I was working the entrance door one night a month later when two, young, attractive women walked in. One looked to be in her early twenties; the other, a little younger. I couldn't take my eyes off of the younger woman. *She is beautiful!* When I carded them, I discovered they were actually sisters, and the younger girl who had captured my attention was only 16 years old. Her I.D. stated that her first name was Erica.

Big sister batted her eyes coyishly. "Would you let her in with me? Please?"

What could it hurt? She is with her sister, and they are both so beautiful. Maybe one of them would at least give me a dance during my shift break.

My eyes darted left and right. "Okay," I conceded. "I'll do it because she is with you, but I'm going to keep an eye on her to make sure she stays safe."

I certainly wasn't going to mind the assignment. There was just something about Erica that drew my full attention. She walked in a regal manner, like she was somehow untouched by the world and needed to be protected. With her long black hair and cocoa-colored skin, she looked like the depictions writers had used when describing Cleopatra. Part black, part Asian, and part Native American, Erica was a knockout and totally out of my league, but I began to dream of somehow having a future with this girl who had decided to break the law and go disco dancing with her older sister.

Yet Erica was so sweet, so naïve, that I almost felt I should not pursue her at all because I would surely just mess up her life. I dared to think, *Maybe she is the miracle God is sending to help save me from myself and the bad decisions I have been making.*

As crazy as it sounds, I felt myself instantly and helplessly falling in love with a 16-year-old girl that I had just met.

Later in the evening, I went over to see how the duo was doing. I looked at Erica. She was even more beautiful up close. Her smile and dreamy eyes smote me.

So did her lack of response. I tried to talk to her then, and several other times that night, but she didn't seem at all interested in me. Finally, I asked something that had to solicit a reply.

"Could I please have your phone number?"

"Well, I am a high school senior, and—" About all I heard after that was *humma, humma, humma,* but she was basically saying, "Thank you—but no, thank you." She was very sweet, and she didn't mean to hurt my feelings, but I was so disappointed. Erica would later say that she remembered meeting me that night, but that the most she could recall was that she thought I was cute. She was just there to have fun with her sister.

"I understand," I replied, and went back to my bouncer duties at the podium near the entrance. After making my rounds through the parking lot, I saw Erica and her sister getting ready to head home for the night, and decided fortune favors the bold.

I asked her sister, who lived in Louisville and just happened to be visiting Erica, for their home phone number—and I got it! Erica was distracted and had no idea she had given it to me.

I suppose her sister must have realized that there was more to it than just me wanting to dance with a cute girl. I was shocked and thrilled that she gave me the number at all.

Two days later, I called it, engaged in brief conversation with Erica's sister, and casually inquired if Erica was home and if she could speak with me.

There was some preliminary small talk. "Do you remember me?" I asked.

She said she did.

"Are you sure you don't maybe want to be friends?" I followed.

"No, I can't," she replied very nicely, "but, again, thank you."

In my mind, Erica never completely told me "no." It's not like she had said, "I don't want to be bothered by you," or "Dude, stop calling me!" Today, Erica says it was simply that she wasn't looking for any sort of relationship at that moment.

I hung up, and I knew I should just let it go. But I couldn't.

I was playing basketball at a nearby park two days later and came across a girl who turned out to be one of Erica's friends at school.

"Are you the bouncer guy from the disco that Erica met a few days ago?"

I said "yes," and she then told me something that changed my life forever.

"Erica likes you," she declared, "but she's just really shy!"

In reality, Erica says she told her exactly what she had told me on the phone—but you know how friends can be.

It was all I needed. From that moment on, I went into full stalker—ur, I mean, research—mode. I found out where Erica lived. I learned when her school day ended. I was Magnum P.I., and I was hot on the case.

A couple of days afterward, I stopped by Erica's house, timing my mid-afternoon visit with when I knew she'd be home from school. I knocked, and she answered.

Go for broke, Magnum!

Without saying a word, I swiftly leaned forward and gave her a kiss.

Erica was in such shock she did not kiss me back, but she didn't push me away, either. In retrospect, it must've been incredibly awkward for her, and it was definitely a bit rash on my part. But, hey, it was certainly memorable. Erica totally wasn't expecting it and didn't know whether to be offended or scared, but she now realizes that I always moved fast while she preferred to go in slow motion.

She quickly gathered her wits. "You need to leave. My father will be home soon."

I was too giddy to care. "I'll be back," I promised, then declared, "I love you, and I am going to pursue you and meet your parents. I'm going to do whatever it takes to win you over."

That I did, and in the most unusual of ways, but those stories are still to come.

My decision to go after Erica was significant because of what she would become—my soulmate and life partner—as well as what she *didn't* do as we began spending time with one another. Not once did she mention my face. Today, she says she noticed that my skin looked red, possibly sunburned, was oily, and appeared to be a bit irritated, but it didn't faze her. She still thought I was cute.

At that stage of my life, I thought I was ugly. I questioned whether or not I'd ever meet someone, especially after what had happened with my fiancé. I was convinced that all the cards were stacked against me.

Erica changed that, and that, in turn, started to change how I felt about myself and what I believed I could ultimately become.

> I was convinced that all the cards were stacked against me.

Still, one more change was required. I needed to make an eternal change so I could fully overcome myself. That came when I was 22 years of age. By then, Erica and I were married, we had our first child, a baby girl, and we had been to Germany and back after my first overseas tour in the Army.

While growing up, my previous church experiences, dating all the way back to the little Methodist church Big Mama took us to every Sunday in Jefferson Town, Kentucky, had given me opportunities to hear about God and the Bible. After completing basic training in the Army and during my advanced individual training, I had opted to attend church services on Sundays to reduce the probability of kitchen duty. When I went, I had listened to what was being taught.

But I had never made a formal decision to become a born-again Christian.

In truth, I was very much a lost soul when I was stationed at Ft. Knox, as evidenced by my behavior. Then, after meeting and eventually marrying Erica, I started seriously thinking about the condition of my soul. In church, I had heard about how I needed to be the head of the house, the spiritual leader of my family. I realized I wanted to be there for Erica and our children, like Big Daddy had been for me in place of my absent father. I also wanted to make sure my family went to church like Big Mama had done for us as I grew up.

All of that was on my mind as Erica and I were assigned to Herzogenaurach, Germany for a year, during which time our first daughter was born. We were on Herzo Base, a German airfield that was used during World War II and later repurposed as a U.S. Army artillery base. I had asked to be assigned there because my brother, with whom I'd had a love-hate-love relationship throughout our upbringing, was already stationed there, and I wanted to be closer to him. Herzo Base was small, with a couple of old barracks and a few newer Army buildings to house and service the current military contingent, but it had an unusable airfield and was situated on beautiful, green countryside. My duties there involved working as a field artillery soldier, computing the firing data to ensure the artillery rounds landed at the correct coordinates.

On Sundays, though, Erica and I occasionally went to church at a military chapel that met in a Quonset hut building on base. With wooden pews and mostly void of decoration, the chapel housed a basic Protestant service for all comers regardless of denominational background or preference. Sometimes we attended more out of a sense of obligation than anything else, and we didn't do it as much as we should have. But we went anyway, knowing that it was the right thing to do. I wasn't trying to have an actual relationship with God. I was just checking the box.

We returned to the United States in the summer of 1982 so I could undergo additional missile maintenance systems-related training at the Redstone Arsenal Army post in Huntsville, Alabama. I had progressed during my tour in Germany to a bona fide leader in the Army as a non-commissioned officer directly responsible for men, equipment, and missions. There were nine pay grades, each one coming with more responsibility and accountability, and I had made it all the way up to the fifth level.

It was also at Redstone Arsenal that I switched my military occupational skill (MOS) from artillery to missile system maintenance—and it was at Redstone that I met Greg. An Army missile systems instructor, Greg was also a Baptist minister who took it upon himself to mentor me during breaks in my training. He noticed how I corrected others when they cussed in class and how I calmed down negative behavior. Greg perceived that I was an informal leader that people would follow, but he saw something else, too.

"You ought to make a decision to serve the Lord," he'd tell me. "I can see that you were raised right. I can see that you're trying to do right." He kept bugging me about it, and as he did,

I'd come home after work and say to Erica, "Greg is my teacher, and he is a nice guy. He means well. But he is getting on my last nerve."

Then, one afternoon, Greg added an invitation to his plea. "I'll come to your house."

You know what? I thought. *I'll have him come and talk to us. What do I have to lose?*

I set it up with Greg for later that night. When I told Erica about it, she wasn't against my decision, but she wasn't excited about it, either. That was mostly because of where we lived. Not a house at all, it was a tiny, lower income apartment we not-so-affectionately called "the roach motel." Located right outside one of the main gates, it had a teeny-weeny galley kitchen just inside the entrance that opened into our combo "living room-bedroom-whatever else we could make it" room. A mini bathroom hid in the back corner. Next to our bed was our main piece of furniture: a dingy, wooly, brown plaid couch.

Everything was cast into a dim glow by amber overhead lights that, sadly, did nothing to obscure the cockroaches that wouldn't go away no matter how often we deep cleaned or bombed the place with insecticide. They had infested the entire apartment complex and returned to every nook and cranny of our apartment as fast as we could chase them way.

It was all that we could afford, and Erica and I both thought it was a little embarrassing and not at all suitable for visitors. Nevertheless, we set up a time for Greg to stop by, and we did our best to make "the roach motel" presentable for an Army instructor and minister.

Greg arrived, and we sat together at our little dining table and shared pound cake and coffee. It went well, and Greg didn't at all act like he was uncomfortable or offended to be in our humble hovel. After we finished, we moved over to the adjacent room. Greg and I sat on the couch while Erica perched herself on the edge of the bed. Next to her, our daughter was asleep in her crib at the foot of the bed.

Carefully and with compassionate deliberation, Greg took the next couple of hours to tell us about Jesus and how God could turn my life around. Erica, who was raised as a Catholic, listened politely, and saw that Greg was kind, sincere, and was trying to help me. She could tell that Greg was talking to her, too, but she also sensed that the minister discerned that she wasn't really understanding what was going on. Even though she had been to church with me many times before, knew about God, and believed He existed, she was not at a point of decision at that moment.

Greg took us through the story of Joseph in the book of Genesis—who, you'll later learn, had been a favorite Bible character of mine from childhood. Joseph was the young man who had been sold into slavery by his brothers and was falsely accused and imprisoned before becoming a leader under the Pharaoh in Egypt.

I had always resonated with Joseph. I had been the "white" black sheep of my family. I was the burden, the embarrassment, the stranger in a strange land. Like Joseph, I felt I'd experienced my share of unfairness, beginning with my parentage and continuing through my three fiery losses. Yet now, like Joseph, I knew I was being called to lead, both in the military and at home.

Somewhere in the course of our discussion with Greg, it hit me that Jesus was real and that I needed to make a full commitment to serve God. Greg asked, "Where would you go tonight if you died? Be honest, Harry. Where would you go?"

My immediate thought was of something harrowingly familiar to me.

Fire.

I pictured the smoke and brimstone of hell itself and thought of what I knew it meant from all those messages I'd heard in church: eternal separation from God. I also reflected, *I have progressed so far in my life, but I need to go to that next level where I'm not a victim anymore. I want to be a victor, not a victim. The only way for me to be a victor is through Jesus.*

Finally, I realized that my decision was going to be all about becoming a leader, and leading my home, as a Christian man. It was one thing to be a leader in the military. It was a greater responsibility and challenge to be the leader of my family.

Greg asked me to pray with him, and I invited Jesus to forgive my sins and to come into my life. Greg then did a great job of explaining how the Christian life was not easy but a gradual process of asking for help, guidance, and strength to become the person God had purposed me to be.

Just as I had done with Erica, I moved fast, and I was all in.

In my heart and mind, and with all my emotions and logic, I became a Christian.

I sold out for God—and began what has been a lifelong journey of overcoming myself so that I could be all that I could be as a leader and a servant to others.

Obstacles of an almost-thwarted birth, a racially taboo heritage, a tough upbringing, injuries and fires, and a misguided early adulthood all had to be overcome to set me on a path to purpose and success.

In *A Flawed Man's Plans in God's Hands*, Erica and I will share more stories and details from our incredible, unpredictable lives with the goal of inspiring you to discover and live a better, fuller life with fewer flaws and more joy. At the close of this book, Erica and I will unveil four essential discoveries and eight final truths that you can learn and apply. Our intention also is that you will learn to forgive yourself and others along the way on your journey through life!

In the end, it is our hope that we will encourage and equip you to be an overcomer and take the lead!

You can succeed even though you started out in poverty.

You can have a long-term marriage even though you come from a broken home.

You can give back even though others have taken from you.

You *can*—if you put your plan in God's hands.

Chapter 1

THE PLAN BEGINS TO UNFOLD

I was excited when Big Mama dropped me off one Saturday afternoon at my friend Tony's house to play. He was a white boy, and we were third grade classmates and best friends. We got along really well, so when she drove me across town to play at his house for the first time, I couldn't have been happier. In a hurry to get to an appointment, she didn't come in then to meet his parents, but they welcomed me, making sure we had Little Debbie snack cakes while we played soldiers all afternoon in the backyard at his beautiful home.

When Big Mama returned that evening to pick me up, she parked her car and came inside to apologize to Tony's parents for rushing off earlier that day without saying hello to them. As they conversed, my friend's mother and father came to realize that Big Mama was not the black nanny they had presumed her to be, but my maternal grandmother.

Suddenly, I wasn't their son's white friend from school.

I was the half-black boy from the wrong side of the tracks.

That night, they angrily told their son that I could never come to their home again. They also didn't want him to have anything else to do with me at school.

Unaware that anything was wrong, I returned to school Monday morning. After roll call, we went to our cubbies to put away the stuff we couldn't keep at our desks, and Tony came up to me. I could tell he had been crying.

"Harry, I've got to talk to you."

"What's wrong?" I asked.

"I know you're my best friend, but we can't be friends anymore. You can't come over to my house again, either."

"Why? What happened?"

"My parents don't like it because you are part black. My dad doesn't want us to be seen together because it could cause other people to get upset where we live if you and your family members kept coming over, unless they were cleaning the house or doing the lawn work or whatever."

I was totally confused. "Did I do something wrong?"

"No," he quickly answered, then turned to go back to his desk.

I just stood there a moment, tears welling up in my own eyes. *Why?*

That night, I tried to explain what had happened to Big Mama and Big Daddy. I waited until dinner had been cleaned up and everybody else had gone on to whatever they were doing. I didn't want to get judged by my other family members.

Big Mama and Big Daddy were having coffee by themselves at the kitchen table. I pulled out a chair across from them and sat down. "Big Mama," I said, "my friend doesn't want me to come over anymore."

She looked at me over the rim of her cup. "Why? I thought everything went well."

"It did, but he found out that I live with a black family."

Her expression said it all. Her brow furrowed and her lips pressed together in stern agitation. Big Daddy sighed and shook his head.

"Well," she replied with a sassy edge, "you don't need that type of friend anyway. You got to watch out for white people. You are different. You will never be like them. You just have to get used to it. That's just the way it is."

"But I was elected class president earlier this year. People seem to like me at school. Tony was my friend. I don't understand."

Big Mama didn't reply. She just got up and stormed off. That made me feel bad. I hadn't wanted to upset Big Mama. Big Daddy got up, too, but he didn't pursue her. Instead, he walked over to me, reached down, and gave me a huge hug.

"It will be alright, Harry. Everything will work out."

As I cried in Big Daddy's arms, I thought back to a couple of years earlier when all of us were visiting with our extended family out in the country in Bloomfield, Kentucky. I was holding hands with my grandfather as we walked together to the general store to get some supplies. Big Daddy was a very dark-skinned man, so my very white appearance was quite a contrast for anyone who observed us.

As we turned down an aisle, we were approached by some of his friends in Bloomfield.

"Why are you walking around with that little white boy?" one of them asked derisively.

I wanted to hang my head, but Big Daddy looked down at me before I could, then turned his gaze to the speaker. Normally the strong, silent type, his brow furrowed, and his eyes got wide, an expression that meant he was angry. Even his mustache seemed to quiver as he responded.

"What are you talking about? He's my grandson! You had better not say anything else bad about him or how he looks."

I was so proud of my grandfather for the way he loved, validated, and protected me that day—and I couldn't help but feel the same way that night in his arms at the kitchen table.

From that moment onward, everything was different between Tony and me. We'd see each other, wave or nod, and sometimes engage in small talk, but that was it. In the weeks that followed, as I processed the essential fact that I had lost my first real best friend from school, another reality set in. *Whoa. I am somewhere in the middle of this color line. I'm black. I'm white. I'm both. What exactly am I?* It was uncomfortable, and with everything else that had happened in my young life, it was just one more rock to lug around in my identity rucksack.

I had always known that I was different from others in my family, and it would still be another few years before I really heard and understood the term "biracial."

But I was beginning to see what it actually meant.

Such racism not only reared its ugly head when I went across town or elsewhere in Louisville, but it was also the case in the predominately black part of Louisville where I grew up. I began to notice how inconvenient and costly it was for my family. It was inconvenient because of how my mere appearance drew unwanted attention in a time when many people of color were trying to get by in society as quietly as possible. As a result, I always had to be explained to others by my Big Mama or Big Daddy. Not everyone was nasty about it. There were kind inquiries such as, "Who is he?" or "Why do you have him?" that my grandparents handled with patience and care. But it seemed to me like there was an inquisition every time we went out.

Today, I can only imagine how tiring that became after a while for Big Mama, Big Daddy, and other members of my family. I'm sure there were times it would have been easier for them to just not have me out in public at all, and believe me, I was just fine staying home and not feeling targeted as well.

My presence at home was costly because there I was, my black mother in a mental health facility and my white father long gone. I was just another body to clothe and another mouth to feed. It also cost my grandparents, aunt, uncle, and other extended family members all the time and energy it took to integrate somebody like me into their all-black family. My appearance caused pain and embarrassment to my family, and especially to my siblings, because though I had a white father I had never met, they all had the same black father who had also abandoned them. He had left our mother before I was born.

To this day, I don't know the full story, but I certainly don't blame any of them now for not accepting me as a full brother. That's one of the reasons why I have spent my entire adulthood trying to build better relationships with my family. There were up to 15 of us living together at any given time in our small house. It must've been hard for the adults to help me try to fit in, especially with all of the kids. The challenges my family experienced just having me around were ever present.

> The challenges my family experienced just having me around were ever present.

When I was eight, I joined one of my cousins, and my brother who was closest to me in age, in regularly going to the area YMCA to play basketball, flag football, and other sports for a couple of years, and that may have made things a bit easier on everyone. Going to the YMCA was an escape, and I loved it. The leaders and coaches there always made me feel welcome and included.

There was one coach, Mr. Bob, who I will never forget. A white man in his early thirties with curly black hair and in fantastic athletic shape, Mr. Bob had a way of making me feel like I wasn't just an accident that others had to deal with. He was one of the first people, other than Big Daddy, who built up my self-esteem. He was also an awesome role model who made me believe, as a biracial person born out of wedlock and with an identity crisis, that I could make a positive difference.

I credit the YMCA, and leaders like Mr. Bob, with helping me begin my dream of becoming successful in life. One December, he even signed me up, along with my brother and cousin, for a program for underprivileged youth on welfare to receive free Christmas gifts from the city. I never forgot that program and how it made me feel, and as an adult, I have been able to institute similar programs in the communities I served both during my military career and today as a leader in my community.

The brother who went with me to the YMCA was the one I mentioned earlier who had a love-hate-love relationship with me. At times, he was very cruel to me with his angry words and harsh actions, and I often felt like he was more embarrassed by me than anything. Still, I did everything I could when I was little to get close to him. He once asked me to get into the driver's seat of Big Daddy's vehicle, a Chevrolet sedan. It was parked in the yard near an old white table we used when we wanted to eat outside.

I walked over, opened the door, and hopped up behind the steering wheel, wondering what my brother had in mind.

"Harry," he said, nodding toward the dashboard. "Do you see that button?"

I nodded. Our grandfather's vehicle had one of those old-fashioned push button ignition switches that wouldn't completely turn over the engine but caused the car to move forward a few inches each time the button was pressed.

"Push it, Harry. Let's see what happens."

Eager to please, I did what he said over and over, slowly going forward each time until I ran into the table and broke two of its legs.

My grandfather was out back and heard the commotion. He came around and slowly walked to the car, opened the door, and asked me to get out. He looked sad, but I wasn't at all afraid of what Big Daddy was going to do. It was how Big Mama was going to react that had me on edge. Of course, I got what I was supposed to get in terms of punishment. My brother acted like he was all innocent.

That was the first time I understood that I couldn't allow myself to do things that I shouldn't in order to try to be accepted by others, even my brother. Looking back, I get it. Neither one of us ever knew our fathers. He had been abandoned like I had been abandoned. We were hurting, and as I've said, hurting people do hurtful things.

But that was just par for the course for young Harry back then, and it didn't get a whole lot better when I was at school. I attended three different elementary schools. There was Bashford Manor, the racially integrated school where I had been voted third grade class president before the incident with Tony's parents. The other two schools were segregated and all black: Newburg and Booker T. Washington. I attended each of those two schools briefly in the fourth grade during my short stint living in two different locations with my momma, the second of which being the house that burned down.

I learned to do two things well at school: run and fight. I had just started going to school at Booker T. Washington before it became clear that there were some bullies who wanted to do harm to me. Yet I discovered that there was a way to run down the hallway, up the steps, and around the corner so that I didn't have to face them. So, once I figured that out, I used that route every day to get to class without being accosted.

If I did get into a fight when I was at school, it was only because I had been goaded into it. I didn't want to fight, but there were several times when someone took a swing at me, I'd dodge it, and give them the counterpunch. I got so good at it that I was like Muhammad Ali doing his famous rope-a-dope in the boxing ring. I never got beat up by anyone.

Until I got home, that is. The only ones who ever succeeded in hitting me and getting away with it were some of my family members. That was because I refused to retaliate against them or tattletale about them to Big Mama. I could have fought back easily, but I couldn't bring myself to do it. My sense of family kept me from fighting back regardless of how I was treated or how often I was hit, particularly by my siblings or cousins. I don't wish to be too accusatory, and I don't want to exonerate their actions, either. But they would hit me, it seemed, for no reason. One of my cousins, who was 10 years older than me, said it happened to me every day, and I often wondered what I could have done to be hit so often by my family members. It was no wonder Big Mama sat me beside her at the dinner table.

There is still pain in my family stemming from all of that. Suffice it to say, I understood being disciplined for doing wrong or being unsafe, but most of the punishment I received from my family was not born out of love or affection, but more from disdain and aggression. I have forgiven them for those actions that they didn't even understand back then. I love my family. All of that is just part of my story, and we all have a story to tell.

I was 11 when I moved back into the nicer home with Big Mama and Big Daddy. I went from growing up in the shotgun house with no utilities to a five bedroom, two bath, red brick home with indoor plumbing and electricity. We actually had toilets inside the house, including one in the basement where the room that I shared with my brother and younger cousin was located. That bathroom even had a movement sensitive light switch that turned on when I shut the door.

As I sat on the commode opening and shutting the door just to see the light come on and off, I thought the sky was the limit now that I had a better home to live in. It was in a subdivision of Louisville that was somewhat integrated with black and white families, and that excited me. We were less isolated from our neighbors, and the integration made me feel a little less out of place. The roads were newer, and my school was only one block away, so I could walk to and from school safely. The playground was integrated, too, giving me the opportunity to be with different people and learn how they experienced life. I also didn't have to smell pigs or hear trains at all hours of the day and night like I had where I first grew up. It was wonderful.

Another great thing that happened just a few weeks after moving into the new home was when my aunt took me, her youngest son, my next oldest brother, and a close family friend and her two kids to Disney World in Florida! It was totally unexpected, and to this day, I don't know how my family managed to afford such an extravagant vacation. It could only have been made possible by proceeds from the sale of the property for the old house, combined with my aunt saving money from her meager paycheck along with whatever was set aside from the earnings of Big Mama and Big Daddy over a long period of time. I will always be thankful for their sacrifices to allow the trip to happen.

It was only the second year Disney World was open, and that six-day getaway was a huge event in my life. I witnessed with my own eyes a broader view of America where I was able to see other people from many cultures and ethnicities together and having fun. No one even slightly noticed or cared if I was half black or half white. No one was ashamed of me. No one felt the need to apologize for me. Everyone accepted me. I got away from the black and white color line crucible for a few days and enjoyed life at its fullest and funniest! Like the Disney cartoons, there was all of this color, everything was clean, everyone was happy, and the birds were singing. I met and spoke to Winnie the Pooh—and Tigger, too! I was pinching myself. I couldn't believe it all.

More than that, it was on that trip to Disney World that I was able to speak with many people from different ethnicities, and every one of them made me feel like I had worth and that my comments were both accepted and respected. We were standing in line for the "It's a Small World" ride, and a white gentleman and his family were there. I was at the back of my family's place in line, and he was behind me at the front of his family's place.

"How is your trip going?" he asked, and we started making small talk. At some point, he asked me what I wanted to do when I grew up.

"I'm going to travel the world and be a soldier," I declared. "I want to help people."

"That's interesting," he replied with all sincerity. "I'm sure you'll be good at that!"

During the trip, my aunt took note of my communication skills, seeing that I could hold an intelligent conversation and that I wasn't afraid to speak with people from different cultures. That was a far cry from the rest of my family who struggled to speak with folks who weren't black. For example, we went out to eat at a couple of restaurants, and at one of them I had a great talk with a guy from India. It was easy for me.

As we drove back home from Florida, my brother, my cousin, and my aunt's friends' kids gave me more respect and consideration than they had on the way there. That was a much different experience than on the way to the park when one of the close family friends' boys decided to push my head into the bathroom wall while we were at a rest stop. His mom really got on him for doing that, and I sat in the front of the sedan after that for the remainder of the trip there.

In all, the Disney World trip proved to be a separation point for me. It showed me that I could operate on a grander scale, and I wasn't going to be confined by my economic situation, being fatherless, or feeling out of place. I was not going to be condemned to live a life of always having to say I was sorry for my very existence.

That was not going to be my story.

When I returned to daily life after the trip, I possessed a new self-confidence and a hope for life that I did not previously have. Something within me told me that I *was* going to travel the world and even be asked to speak to large groups of people about important subjects. That was when I joined the Boy Scouts at age 12, and within two years, I began speaking at camping jamborees in front of hundreds of boys and adults about scouting culture and laws and about what scouts did to help the community. By the time I was 13, I was asked to speak on the life of Jesus when our Methodist church hosted denominational conferences. I focused on Christ's teachings about, and His interactions with, children, such as those in Matthew 18 and 19. I also spoke on how we should give back to our children and show patience and love for them. I was even asked to recite Christian-based poetry that I had written.

Our neighborhood had kid's clubs that began to place their trust in me as a leader, organizer, or money manager. One was a bicycle group, about a dozen of us, that rode to certain places and played sports with different teams. Our sign was a "thumbs up," like Fonzie from the TV show, *Happy Days*. For example, if we thought someone in the club was telling a lie, we'd ask, "Are you telling the truth? Thumbs up!"

Just like that, I was no longer being pushed to the rear. In fact, it almost felt like I was intentionally being moved to the forefront. I now believe that was God working and speaking into my life to show me what my future was going to hold as a leader.

> Just like that, I was no longer being pushed to the rear.

I also attended summer Vacation Bible School at Green Acres Baptist Church. All of the teachers were white men or women. That was a brand new experience for me, and they were awesome. I was likely more easily accepted at the Vacation Bible School than I was in the black educational system because I looked more white than black, though when the teachers found out that I was actually biracial, they were surprised but continued to treat me well. The only variation to that came one morning on the Vacation Bible School bus when one of the church monitors was convinced that I was on the wrong bus. She thought I should have been on the white kid's bus instead of the one that went into my neighborhood. By then, having others believe I should've been just another one of the white kids had become a normal occurrence.

My primary Sunday School teacher at the Vacation Bible School was a successful white businessman named Gene. An unassuming medium-sized, medium-built man in a crisp suit shirt and tie, Mr. Gene became bigger than life to me. He was articulate, very versed in the Bible, had great classroom management skills, and was always well prepared. He rewarded his students if they made a good effort, and he created a safe, positive environment for all of us. A passionate man, I could tell that Mr. Gene truly cared about the souls of all of his students, as did his wife who worked on the school's staff. He greeted me with a smile and a hug every day of that two week Vacation Bible School, and I had never experienced that much love and attention in such a short period of time from anyone outside of my aunt and grandparents.

Mr. Gene allowed me to read Scripture verses aloud during our study period, and on our fun breaks he talked to me about what I wanted to do when I became an adult. Just as I had with the man at Disney World, I told him my aspirations, and Mr. Gene told me he knew I would be good at whatever I became.

"You are an awesome teacher," I told him on one of those fun breaks, "and one day I'd like to teach as well." Then I added, "I want to be like you and wear a suit. I want to be respected. I want a wife who supports me, and I will support her." I knew that because Mr. Gene and his wife had modeled to me what that looked like.

I couldn't wait to go to Vacation Bible School, and Mr. Gene was a big reason for that. A successful businessman like him telling me I would be successful as an adult? It was amazing.

I also enjoyed my classmates. I had a very diverse class, and we all got along great. Once again, I didn't have to explain my ethnicity to anyone, and no one made me feel bad about being half black/half white, born out of wedlock, and not living with my parents. In addition, it was at Vacation Bible School that my faith began to develop, not only in God, but also in my fellow human beings. To a certain extent, I had been raised to think that white men in particular were essentially bad and not to be trusted, but I saw that there were good and bad people in all races.

As I began moving to the forefront, experiencing and perceiving what I could become, it had an unexpectedly negative impact on my siblings and cousins. As a kid, one of my favorite characters in the Bible was Joseph. His story, told in Genesis 37-50, started with his father, Israel, making a colorful coat for Joseph. His brothers believed that their father loved Joseph more than them, and they hated him so much that they could not speak a kind word to him. Not long after that, Joseph had a dream that he told his brothers about. The dream made them hate him all the more.

"We were binding sheaves of grain out in the field," Joseph said, "when suddenly my sheaf rose and stood upright, while your sheaves gathered around mine and bowed down to it."

His brothers didn't like the implications. "Do you intend to rule over us?" they accused.

Later, Joseph told them of another dream. In it, the sun, moon, and 11 stars (indicative of his 11 brothers) bowed down to him.

In these dreams, the Lord was showing Joseph a future where he would indeed be a ruler, even over his entire family. But his brothers did not accept any of it. They became jealous to the point that they took Joseph into the desert, stripped him of his colorful coat, and threw him into a cistern. Shortly after that, they sold Joseph to a group of people in a caravan heading for Egypt. After the caravan left, the brothers dipped Joseph's coat in animal's blood, went home, and told their father that Joseph had been killed.

Obviously, I had no desire to become a ruler over my siblings and cousins. But it certainly seemed that I was being pushed ahead of them toward leadership. I was going to be something they felt they could not be. By no fault of my own, and with no ill intent, I was starting to increase in a way they never thought I would—and it seemed like some of them became a bit jealous of me as a result. When I was in the Boy Scouts, I was promoted faster than my brother, the same one who had gotten me in trouble with Big Daddy's Chevrolet, and the other kids in our troop from our neighborhood, including the boy who had pushed my head into a wall on the way to Disney World. I was put in charge of both of them, and they didn't like it at all.

"Who are you to be in charge?" they teased. "What gives you the right?"

Then we had a camping trip. I showed them how to properly set up the camp site, led them on hikes, and helped them with tasks such as tying knots. I ate up the opportunity to be in charge, and I did everything I could to lead by example. When our outing was over and it was time to leave, they did everything they were told without complaint, and I could tell something had changed. From then on, they treated me better, and I felt validated.

Still, a gap was growing between me and my siblings and cousins that I didn't create or want, but it was there, nonetheless. As many influential people, both white and black, began to invest in me with their knowledge and encouragement, and as I experienced being treated differently by society in general, it was palpable. I could feel it, and my family could, too. I'm not saying my other family members didn't receive encouragement from influential community leaders, but the input that I received was broader because it came from both sides of the color line.

People went out of their way to ensure they gave me a good word. In addition to Mr. Gene at Vacation Bible School, my scoutmasters, Jim and Alan, impressed upon me the ideals of responsibility and honesty, which taught me the importance of character. Another man, a wealthy, white physician, Dr. Handmaker, informed my perspective about education. My aunt was a nanny to his children, and I sometimes accompanied her when she went to his home. One visit, Dr. Handmaker observed me looking at his medical degree on the wall. He asked me what I wanted to be when I grew up.

"I want to be a soldier and a leader," I declared.

"You're smart, Harry," he affirmed. "You can become a doctor one day, too."

So many people poured into me, exhorting me to set my expectations higher. One summer, I was selected by a gentleman in Louisville Parks and Recreation to be the supervisor for clean up at a local park. It was only a temporary job, but I felt so humbled to be the leader over several boys I had grown up with who, in previous years, wouldn't listen to anything I had to say. When one of them, one of my best childhood friends, showed up late for work, I even docked his pay for the time he missed.

My tendency toward rigidity as a leader was showing itself even then, but he remains a friend today.

As part of that job, I was also responsible for a free food giveaway program for lower income kids. The food was delivered to the park, I made sure it was distributed fairly, and then my crew and I handled the clean-up. One afternoon, as I watched over the kids while they played, a little six-year-old girl was going down the slide, and she began to choke. She had a coin in her mouth, and it was blocking her esophagus.

I ran over, grabbed the girl off the slide by her ankles, turned her upside down, and shook her as hard as I could. Within seconds, the coin dislodged, and she spit it out onto the ground. That was the first time in my life that I was able to respond quickly to help someone that was under duress and in trouble. I credit my Boy Scout training, and of course, the grace of God that allowed me to save the little girl from possibly choking to death. From that day forward, I became more than aware of the safety of other people. That was the lynchpin event that led to me receiving several safety awards years later in the Army. I remain beyond safety conscious.

Later that day, the little girl's mother came up to thank me for what I had done, and a news reporter interviewed me about the incident. A few days later, one of my friends told me his parents had read about it in the newspaper. It was a big deal, and I was made out to be a hero. I suppose I was one, though I only did what any good Eagle Scout should do. Yet when I went home to tell my family about it, no one, not even Big Mama or Big Daddy, seemed to fully believe me. There was this general feeling that I was making the whole thing up. Even after I mentioned the news reporter, it didn't make a difference.

I was the dreamer, the kid that talked about being a soldier and traveling the world someday, and I believe they were too busy trying to survive to listen to me.

———

I was still active in church and in the Boy Scouts when a combination of influences—envious family members, peer pressure, and good old-fashioned hormones—drew me toward a series of destructive decisions that tainted my late teenage years.

I played both football and soccer in high school, and I began smoking marijuana after football practice with a couple of my friends. That started a periodic habit that continued through the rest of my high school days. One day, a friend and I were in the smoking area of the school courtyard. It was tucked off in a corner outside the cafeteria and had a couple of picnic tables, trees, and hedges. He pulled out a joint, and we took turns smoking it, never noticing the teacher who walked up on us. I was about to take a toke when I saw him, and I quickly threw the joint into the bushes. The teacher gave us a long lecture on the woes of smoking drugs, but I was too high to remember exactly what he said. All I knew was that I hated getting caught.

Away from school, our neighborhood clubs got older and a bit more raucous. We weren't gangs by any stretch of the imagination. We didn't have any weapons. But fights sometimes broke out between us if we felt we needed to avenge someone or protect what we saw as our territory. There were times when it was serious business, and all hands were on deck. One such time happened one hot, sunny Saturday afternoon when my club was playing a tackle football game against another club at the elementary school playground. We didn't usually tackle each other too hard, but it was warm, and tempers were getting frayed in the heat of competition. A big, dark-skinned kid on the other team, who just happened to be a longtime sports rival at school, put in a little extra pizzazz when he tackled one of my teammates, and I didn't like it.

Running up next to him while he was still on top of my teammate, I ducked a punch and got in a swing before some of the other players pulled us apart. We were grunting and shouting, and my rival called me a few foul and creative racial names as we were separated. That was nothing new. He'd always called me names, but I didn't return the verbal fire. I never used such monikers against people of color, no matter what they said about me. In fact, during high school I was given the nickname "Average White Boy," or AWB. It came from the popular music group, the Average White Band, and it was based on the idea that I may look white, but I wasn't your average white boy. It was like a term of endearment. My coaches called me AWB, and I even had a hat made with the initials that I still have hanging in my closet.

Then there were girls. It was during my sophomore year that, for some reason, they really began to like me. These were the same girls who had laughed at me as they teased me for wearing hand-me-down clothes and styling a buzz top haircut when I was younger. But after Big Mama let me grow my hair out in a curly afro reminiscent of what Prince was sporting at the time, I started attracting their attention. Of course, the angry, devil-may-care expression I usually wore on my face, along with my unusual multiracial skin color, may have had something to do with it. I was also doing well in sports and becoming a leader in school groups, such as the student advisory committee, human relations council, and student council, and through activities like drama club. I filled major roles in two of the four biggest plays we presented: Napoleon in Animal Farm, and the Tin Man in the Wizard of Oz.

In the black culture where I grew up, it was almost expected that kids my age would have premarital sex, so the peer pressure to do so was strong. Yet because I did not want to have a child outside of marriage, I always used contraception, whether my partners did or not. My attitude was simple: I could not father a child who would grow up out of wedlock and unwanted like me.

So, whatever it was that drew them to me, several girls began approaching me to have sex with them. When I was a sophomore, I was asked by a black senior to cut class and meet her at her house. At first, I thought she couldn't be serious and was only making fun of me. But when I arrived, I quickly realized she was serious—and I had no problem complying with her request.

> I could not father a child who would grow up out of wedlock and unwanted like me.

She later told me why she was attracted to me. "I love your hair, but you're different from most other boys." When I pressed her to explain, she mentioned things like self-confidence, my demeanor, and the fact that I didn't seem to be afraid of failure. It was extremely affirming to know that her attraction to me wasn't just about my skin color or hairstyle. It wasn't just about sex. There was another dynamic going on.

My more common sexual experiences in high school were random. One white girl saw me walking down the street in her neighborhood after I had gotten lost trying to find a friends' house. She asked me to come in her home, one thing led to another, and we ended up having sex. It didn't seem to matter who the girl was or what her racial or social background happened to be. Strangely, just as I had been gaining value and enjoying recognition from individuals from all races in other areas of my life, the same thing was happening with girls. They saw me worthy to have sex with them.

To be sure, I am not proud of such promiscuous encounters today. In the Bible, Proverbs 7 presents a discourse warning against the "adulterous woman." Verses 1-5 gives the directive. "My son, keep my words and store up my commands within you. Keep my commands and you will live; guard my teachings as the apple of your eye. Bind them on your fingers; write them on the tablet of your heart. Say to wisdom, 'You are my sister,' and to insight, 'You are my relative.' They will keep you from the adulterous woman, from the wayward woman with her seductive words." Obviously, I did not follow that directive then—but it has certainly informed my actions since. I never felt I was any better or worse than any person that I had sex with. I did not blame those "adulterous" women for our actions. I was just as "adulterous" as them, and we were all lost in our depravity. As an adult, I've actually spoken to many of those women to apologize for my actions, and we have forgiven one another while knowing only God could possibly forgive us.

But back then, I took it for all it was worth. There were other bad behaviors, too. Drinking. Stealing. Pornography. Keeping secrets about what I was doing. I was full of myself and being led by the stuff of life. I do not make excuses for any of my destructive choices based on my unfortunate circumstances or because I was abandoned by my father. It was more a case of me trying to find my way in the world and taking advantage of situations when someone wanted to show me affection. I was just so happy when someone desired being with me that I almost felt obligated to reciprocate their affection.

I even allowed it all to overcome the personal faith that I had started to build. There was no specific event that made me think that God and church were no longer relevant. It was a little bit of this and a little bit of that. I was drawn away. I was riding the fence. I tried to live in two worlds, attempting to fit in so I could have friends and be accepted while still going to church, reading Scripture, and trying to live the Christian life. I was attempting to stay above the fray—but I was living a double life that could not stand. As James 1:5-8 teaches, "If any of you lacks wisdom, you should ask God, who gives generously to all without finding fault, and it will be given to you. But when you ask, you must believe and not doubt, because the one who doubts is like a wave of the sea, blown and tossed by the wind. That person should not expect to receive anything from the Lord. Such a person is double-minded and unstable in all they do."

I was quite unstable, and my choices fueled an identity crisis that, without me knowing it, undermined all the positives that had happened to me—and resulted in a moment of sheer irresponsibility that could've taken my life in an entirely different direction.

Chapter 2

THE PLAN CONTINUES TO UNVEIL

After starting my junior year of high school, I met a girl who was a freshman junior varsity cheerleader. A black girl with thick ebony hair and an athletic build, she had a nice smile that made me feel great about myself, especially when she flashed that smile when she saw me coming her way. A full-on extrovert, she wasn't shy about anything. From the get-go, I could tell she was a very driven person. When she set her sights on something (or someone), she usually got it.

I found out that I was in her sights after she had told some of my friends, in no uncertain terms, that I was going to be her man. My amorous reputation had been growing, so I thought she was simply another girl wanting to sexually experiment with me. She was known to be a good student and a great cheerleader. I was going to be just another encounter to her, nothing more.

Boy was I wrong!

For some reason, she really liked me—so much so that she didn't hesitate to keep pursuing me until we had sex. The football team and cheerleaders often traveled on the same bus to away games, and it was there that she made her intentions plain. She scooched next to me on the seat and leaned in close.

"I'd like to start dating you," she declared, "and if you agree to be my boyfriend, I'll sleep with you right away."

It didn't matter that I told her I wasn't looking for a girlfriend, though I imagine my reputation strongly suggested I wasn't looking for a steady girlfriend anyway. She was undeterred, so I tried another tactic, insisting that we had to use contraception. That was no problem. In fact, she happily announced that she was already on the pill and that I would never have to worry about her getting pregnant.

Like I said, she was driven to get what she wanted—and I was riding the wave of my current popularity that seemed to always result in sex without any emotional attachments.

"We can have sex," I conceded, "but I'm not going to be your boyfriend, at least not in the open. We have to keep it on the down low." She looked older than she was, but I didn't want word to get out about what we were doing because of our age difference.

Victorious, she quickly agreed, and she and I would have sex on and off over the next 18 months. We developed an efficient system. She let me know when her parents weren't going to be home and what time I should come over, and that was it. It couldn't have been any easier, even if I was supposed to be someone else's steady boyfriend during the time I was secretly meeting her at her home.

As we did what we did, it seemed to me that I was just a quick fix for her lack of parental love and affection. She insisted that what we were doing was only about sex. We were just having fun. Yet every time we hooked up, I heard Mr. Gene's voice in my mind quoting Exodus 22:16: "If a man seduces a virgin who is not pledged to be married and sleeps with her, he must pay the bride-price, and she shall be his wife." Mentally, I couldn't keep it casual. I feared that that there would be consequences with this girl that had never occurred to me during my other sexual encounters. I tried to break off the sex with her several times, but the sin and desire were just too strong for me to overcome without Jesus being fully Savior and Lord in my life.

I was a mess—but she and I were two hurting people who wanted to be loved and were using sex as a way to fill the holes in our hearts. I'd discover that she was idealistic and wanted to start her life with someone she felt met her requirements (good hair, light skinned, popular) to be the father of her child. Such traits were valued in the black community because of the prejudice that existed in the predominately white culture that meant a darker colored child would have a harder time than a light skinned child. She also knew that I was a leader at school and was on my way to becoming an Eagle Scout.

I believe it was obvious to her that I would be somewhat successful, so she may have thought she could be the one girl who would tame my wildness and make me settle down and be only with her. She was no doubt encouraged in that perception when my steady girlfriend, who I had started seeing while I was fooling around with her, finally came to her senses and dumped me.

As I became aware that she had actually begun to fall in love with me, I was hoping to find a way to love her back—but there was only lust in my heart. It was truly one of my greatest failures in life. I felt then that I was being transparent and honest with her, but I kept allowing her to have hope that what we had could turn into a lifelong relationship by continuing to spend time with her, all the time knowing that it would not. So, I shouldn't have been as surprised as I was when, in January 1978, she revealed that she might be pregnant and wanted to get married. She said she was ready to be with me for life.

I was 17. She was 15. I knew that what she wanted me to do would be the right, Christian thing to do, but I was running from the Lord. I did not love her, either, and I had always told myself that I would never marry someone unless I really loved them. It was always so sad to me when someone married for anything less than love. I recalled watching classic movies with Big Daddy and dreaming about meeting someone that I would fall in love with on sight who would reciprocate that love just for me.

It may have been corny, but I had grown up with broken marriages and relationships all around me. I did not want to add to that statistic—yet here I was, in a situation to do just that with her. I was such a selfish, hypocritical, unthinking idiot to be destroying a young girl's life like I was. Therefore, when she told me she was pregnant and wanted me to marry her, I responded self-centeredly and ignorantly.

"I am not going to help you raise it because you promised me you were on the pill," I declared. "You are just trying to trap me. I'm your victim!"

"I didn't bend your arm," she retorted in no uncertain terms. "You wanted to do it as much as I did. It is time for you to be responsible and accept that you have a child coming into this world!"

I began to wonder if the child was actually mine or not. I felt I had reason to be suspicious. She and I had stopped having regular sex for a period of time during our 18 month affair, and she had briefly dated another guy that looked similar to me. Paternity tests were becoming easier to access, and I told myself that if I could just make sure the child was really mine, then maybe I'd settle for her, and we'd make a life of it together. But she wouldn't even consider it. She was convinced I was the father of the baby, and that was all there was to it. She confirmed the results of her home pregnancy test at a free clinic.

I was so racked with guilt. I wanted to be a better person, and I truly knew I was living in sin. My mind often went to the words of Revelation 3:15-16, and I applied them to my situation. "I know your deeds, that you are neither cold nor hot. I wish you were either one or the other! So, because you are lukewarm—neither hot nor cold—I am about to spit you out of my mouth." My thoughts and actions were those of a selfish child, and I was about to have a child and damage a young girl's life forever.

It wasn't until much later that I realized I was really the problem, not her. I could have said "no" to her and her advances. I could have walked away and made better decisions for her future and mine. I could have done that, but I didn't. Today, I take full blame for impregnating a girl in her sophomore year of high school, but I sure didn't accept responsibility then.

One reason I had no excuse for my decisions was because I had people in my life that tried to help me do better. My high school principal, Mr. Stanley Whitaker, often checked on me, and several of the other kids of color who may not have had father figures at home. He gave us someone to look up to and emulate. He was a white man called to work with underprivileged kids of color and guide them to successful lives. Mr. Whitaker encouraged me to be the best person I could at all times. He knew I was a Boy Scout, but he could tell that I was battling with peer pressure and self-destructive behavior. He was proud of me for later deciding to join the U.S. Army. He discerned that military service was the best thing for me at that time and would allow me to leave the culture in my neighborhood and give myself a chance to become a better person. Mr. Whitaker remains in my life today and is one of my biggest supporters.

My twelfth-grade home economics teacher, Mrs. Faye Ashworth, constantly told me that I had unlimited potential but needed to find a way to harness my energy in a more positive way. Many of my neighborhood friends had both of their parents to raise them. Most of the time, I had neither, and I could sense that other moms and dads felt a little sorry for me for being so different from those in their communities and always receiving racist remarks from people within my own black community. It was hard for me to see my potential, much less achieve it, despite the fact that several wonderful Christian parents predicted I would be successful in life because they said I was a kid who could be trusted to do the right thing and help others.

At age 17, I was far from the Harry they prophesied, but it really felt good to receive words of affirmation from those parents, and I now realize that God was speaking directly to me through their voices. In Genesis 12:2, the Lord called Abram by proclaiming, "I will make you into a great nation, and I will bless you; I will make your name great, and you will be a blessing." Whenever I remember the encouragement that Mr. Whitaker, Mrs. Ashworth, and those Christian parents spoke into my life, it reminds me of this Scripture as though it were being said of me. Little did I know then that I would one day be able to help hundreds, if not thousands, of people reach their unlimited potential and be their best!

> I could sense that other moms and dads felt a little sorry for me for being so different.

I also didn't take responsibility as I should've for another mistake I made back then. In March, my driver's permit was going to expire. If I didn't renew it, I would have to take the entire test again. I had barely passed it the first time, and I didn't have the money to renew it. On top of that, I was taking driver's education that semester, and I had to have a valid driver's permit to be able to drive.

So, I decided to use a black ink pen to carefully change the "3" to an "8" on my driver's permit so it would appear that it wasn't going to expire until August, allowing me to continue my driver's education class. After I graduated, I went in to renew my permit to give me more time to study for the official driver's license hands-on test. When I gave the clerk my permit, she immediately frowned.

"Did you alter an official state document?" she asked.

My stomach felt rock hard, and my heart pounded. "No, ma'am, I didn't."

Knowing that I was lying, she asked the same question again, and I caved. I reached out and grabbed the counter in front of me to offset my lightheadedness. I was so afraid.

She called over the police officer stationed in the lobby, and I was taken to a room where I had to admit to another lady that I had forged the date. "You'll be receiving a court date to pay a fine for forging an official state document," she stated. I was told to sign several documents before they said I could leave.

A few weeks later, I went to court and paid the $300 fine using money my momma let me borrow from her monthly disability check. Meanwhile, I went to the U.S. Army recruitment office in Louisville to look into joining the military. I had wanted to be a soldier since I was a boy. I loved the idea of joining the Army to see the world, pay for my college education, and grow in a military environment, just like I had in the Boy Scouts. I also assumed that no one would care about my ethnicity or what

I looked like in the Army. I would be evaluated solely on my efforts.

Joining the military was also a way out. Not only was I going to be 18 the summer after I graduated from high school, but I knew I needed to gain an income to be able to pay for the child that was on the way. I also understood that if I joined before my eighteenth birthday, I would receive a bonus, and I needed that extra money more than ever. Finally, I could pay back momma for her help with the fine from my first month of Army pay.

My recruiter was a black man of average height and weight who looked sharp in his uniform and walked into the room with an air of authority and confidence. A very kind person, he took the time to explain the process of joining the Army in a way that made me feel it was definitely the right thing for me, especially considering the position I was in. He told me everything I needed to hear: I'd see the world, defend our country when called upon, and be able to pay my bills, go to college, and support a family if and when I ever got married. I signed my part of the contract that very day.

But there was one problem. Because I was still 17, I needed an adult's signature to validate my contract with the military and seal the deal. That meant I needed to go to my legal guardian, Big Mama. Of course, she knew that I had wanted to be a soldier since I was a child and how well I had done as the only Eagle Scout of color in the history of my Boy Scout district. I thought with all of that going my way, getting her signature so I could join the Army would be an easy slam dunk.

It was anything but that.

"Why don't you just wait until you are eighteen, and you can sign up for yourself?" she replied. "I don't think you should sign up so early. You should wait until you graduate high school and then weigh your options."

I was surprised. Maybe she was hoping I could find a job in Louisville and stick around. Perhaps she was simply concerned for my safety. Or, since she knew I was sexually active and had often warned me of the downfalls of that activity and where it would lead me spiritually, it could be that she wanted to protect me from further activity after I joined the military. I don't know—but I do know Big Mama could tell that the girl I was with wanted to lock me down for life. I didn't tell her anything about the pregnancy, much less how important having a locked-in job and bonus would be to me doing my part to provide for the child.

My grandmother loved me and wanted what she thought was best for me.

She was not going to give me her signature.

Frustrated, I returned to my recruiter to find out what to do next. I shared that my birth mother was in a mental health facility. He said, based on Army guidelines, that her signature would be considered valid to secure permission, despite her state.

A few days later, I went to see her.

"Would you please sign my Army contract so I can have a chance of leaving Louisville and finding my success in life?" I offered.

Momma looked at me with love in her eyes. "I will sign your contract, if you do one thing for me when you join the Army."

"What's that, momma?"

"Be the best soldier you can be," she encouraged. "You were a great Boy Scout, and you'll be a great soldier. I know you'll do well."

As I walked out of the mental health facility with her signature in hand, I should've been thrilled, but I despaired at first. If she knew what else I had been doing in my life—and if she'd known about the girl and the pregnancy—I'm certain it would have saddened her to no end. I did not want momma to know that I was bringing another unwanted child into the world. Of all people, I knew what it felt like to be that child.

I also felt sorry that the facility I was leaving *was* my mother's life, and I couldn't help but wonder if my life was really going to be any better because I was blowing all of my opportunities to do better due to my weakness with sex. I never actually found out if my mother and father actually had a relationship with one another or if he just took advantage of her sexually. Whatever the case, even if sex is consensual, that doesn't necessarily make it right legally, morally, or spiritually. It's just as Ephesians 5:1-3 tells us: "Follow God's example, therefore, as dearly loved children and walk in the way of love, just as Christ loved us and gave himself up for us as a fragrant offering and sacrifice to God. But among you there must not be even a hint of sexual immorality, or of any kind of impurity, or of greed, because these are improper for God's holy people."

But I stuffed away the truth of that Bible passage. Instead, I held my head up. I realized that momma had said all I needed to hear to believe that the Army would be my way to succeed and that I would somehow overcome all of my other weaknesses to become not just a better person—but one of the best soldiers in Army history!

I joined the Army's delayed entry program which allowed me to complete high school before going on active duty that July. My test scores on the Army's Services Vocational Aptitude Battery test, particularly the general technical section score, indicated that I was qualified to attend all Army training for which I was eligible and would get bonus pay if I graduated basic training and matriculated to advanced individual training on time.

Over the next six months, I stayed in touch with the girl as her pregnancy progressed, but we didn't see each other much. I was too busy finishing school and preparing to leave, and too upset that she was not open to us getting a paternity test. At that stage, I had convinced myself it would be proof enough if she placed my name on the baby's birth certificate. But I had already begun separating myself from her—and I had even started dating someone else, someone I did think I could maybe build a life with. We even talked about getting married one day.

At 7:00 a.m. on July 6, one of my older cousins drove me to the Military Entrance Processing Station in downtown Louisville. She wished me well and dropped me off at the front door. I was summarily weighed, measured, fed, and briefed before catching my flight to my basic training site in Ft. Sill, Oklahoma. It was my first ever airplane ride. I was excited to finally be leaving Louisville and beginning my journey as a soldier. At the same time, I didn't want to stay away from home for long, so I ensured that my contract with the Army indicated that I'd be stationed back at Ft. Knox after I completed my basic training, which included field artillery advanced individual training, by late November.

I had never been away from home that long before, but I really enjoyed basic training. I was in the best physical shape of my life, and leadership roles came easily to me. I wasn't selected to be the initial leader of our basic training class, but before long, our drill sergeants and my fellow basic trainees had selected me to be the platoon guide for our unit, the famous artillery training brigade known as "Foxtrot Four." It was my first official leadership position in the Army.

As I trained and led, I received letters and phone calls from the girl back home, keeping me informed about her and the later stages of her pregnancy. She was always warm toward me and kept wanting me to commit to marry her and take care of the baby. In one of our calls, I told her that I would pay child support as needed, but I would not marry her because I did not love her. In another call, I proposed we see a lawyer and go to court to settle everything in a fair and legal way, but she wouldn't consider it. When I did go to an attorney on my own, I was informed that I could not take her to court about paternity. He said that only the mother of the child could do that. So, I felt I had no options left. I would have to wait until the child was born. Through all of this, I tried to be as kind as I could, but she simply would not get the message. She was convinced I was going to change my mind and marry her.

But I wasn't, mostly because of the girl I was now seeing. She was a multiracial girl, part black and part Native American, and she had experienced racism and prejudice similar to what I had. I decided that a marriage was going to work better with someone who was like me in that way. I also told her about the girl who was pregnant, but she was fine with that. She knew that I wanted to be with her while taking responsibility for the child.

The baby was born September 10 after I had completed basic training, and while I was finishing advanced individual training, in Oklahoma as part of Ft. Sill's one station unit training program. When she told me what she had named the baby, I was surprised that his first and middle names had nothing to do with my name. *If she really loves me like she says she does,* my immature mind thought, *why is the child's name so different from mine?* I was so caught up in my own selfishness—though my self-centeredness was tempered a bit after my next phone call with her. That's when she told me that there had been complications with the baby's birth. The umbilical cord had briefly wrapped around the infant's neck, and he had lost oxygen during delivery. The situation was so severe she said the doctor was concerned that long-term physical or mental disabilities were possible as my son got older.

The news that the child I had helped bring into the world may have to deal with such challenges later in life stunned me. How did I feel? I didn't really know—other than being saddened that my lust, my sin, had resulted in a child being born with potential physical or mental challenges, and to a girl that I didn't love. But it did make me realize that I was going to have to make a decision, at some point, to believe in God and His gracious offer of forgiveness or to continue to live in the selfish existence I had created. I had started to hate who I had become, and I was fully realizing that there were real life consequences to my choices. I was 18 years old and overwhelmed with my life and my bad decision making. I was nearing a crossroads, and I felt kind of like the Scarecrow character that I played alongside in my high school play. He didn't know which way to go.

> I was going to have to make a decision, at some point, to believe in God.

I also felt like the Tin Man character that I did portray. He thought he didn't have a heart. *Do I even have a heart myself?* I lamented. I believed God had a begun a work in me back in that Sunday school class with Mr. Gene, and I had to find hope that maybe He could finish it one day, just as Philippians 1:6 promised.

I felt sorry for him and for his mother, knowing that I didn't do anyone any favors by committing the sin of fornication with her, and I prayed for his well-being. Even then, I feared that there would be a reckoning, consequences for my actions, that would come to pass one day. Ezekiel 18 speaks of the sins of the father and how they can impact future generations. That's why 1 Corinthians 6:18-20 declares, "Flee from sexual immorality. All other sins a person commits are outside the body, but whoever sins sexually, sins against their own body. Do you not know that your bodies are temples of the Holy Spirit, who is in you, whom you have received from God? You are not your own; you were bought at a price. Therefore honor God with your bodies."

By the end of November, as per the conditions of my Army contract, I got my first duty assignment to Ft. Knox, moved into a room on the barracks—and drove to Louisville see the baby and his mother. I'd always been good with children. When I was young, most of the smaller children in my extended family took to me very easily, and I loved playing with them, too. I discovered that children do not judge others as quickly or harshly as adults do, so I always felt more comfortable around them. I knew they wouldn't judge me, and they knew I wouldn't judge them.

But while I had loved children growing up, I realized, at this point in my life, that I didn't want to have a child of my own. I did not expect or plan to be raising a child. I was too stupid and selfish to think about such consequences for my actions. Therefore, when I first laid my eyes on my baby boy, I felt as though

I had been cast in a major starring role in a play that I didn't volunteer for, but the show still had to go on.

As I held the child in my arms, I tried to wrap my head around the fact that he was my son. I felt some attachment to the baby, but because of the way he had come into the world under a veil of lies, lust, and guilt, I found it difficult to feel as if this was a wonderful, blessed event. Rather, his presence just solidified the fact that, in his mother, I was going to be attached to someone I did not love for the rest of my life. In addition, I believed I was going to be held hostage mentally, financially, and socially for at least the next 18 years.

Today, I am so ashamed that I felt that way, but to say anything less would not be the truth.

I started making payments to his mother in lieu of official child support after investigating what a reasonable, legal monthly amount would be. Nevertheless, she immediately started dictating when I could spend time with him, with a warning. "You had better not be seeing any other girls. If I find out that you are, you will never see your son again!" I asked her if I could see the birth certificate, and she cruelly sidestepped the request. "Grow up and start taking care of my son. You don't need to see the birth certificate because you should be able to tell he is yours by how he looks!"

As I looked at him lying in his combo baby carrier/car seat, I had hoped he would look like me so I could feel more invested in him and his future, but I didn't think he looked even remotely like me. Still, I conceded, "Hey, I was here enough that the child is probably mine. Different genes are different genes." My last comment was based on a vague recollection from high school biology class that there are dominant and recessive genes that could result in a child not resembling one or both of their parents.

Aggravatingly, his mother would not reveal why she wouldn't let me see the birth certificate. Perhaps it was because she really wasn't sure whose son he was. Maybe she was just being stubborn. I never have found out what her reasons were. I would eventually take a DNA test and verify I was indeed his father—but not until many years later and not long before a tragedy befell him that neither one of us would've ever wanted or dreamed.

In the meantime, my relationship with the other girl came to an abrupt end when I learned that she had started going out with a basketball player from the University of Louisville while I was in basic training and hid it from me. Heartbroken, I stayed away from girls, at least for a few months, until the spring of 1979. That's when I began dating another multiracial girl (she was black, white, and Native American). A year younger than me, she had actually been my date to my senior prom, even though she attended a different high school than I did.

I ran into her at a park in Louisville on one of my weekend visits home from Ft. Knox. I loved going to the park to hang out, play a game or two of basketball with some old high school buddies, and see what was going on. I had just walked off the court when I saw her on the nearby walking trail. I called out her name, she turned around, stopped, and smiled at me. I went over to her, and we reminisced about the neighborhoods we grew up in and about our prom night together. One thing led to another, and we set up a formal date for the following week. She discerned that I was doing okay as a soldier, even if that really wasn't the full truth. I simply tried to put my best foot forward because I was tired of dating around, and I wanted to settle down with someone that I could relate to and share common interests with.

As we continued to date and write letters to one another, not only did I learn that she wanted the same things I did, but I noticed that I was actually becoming a better soldier. Part of it was her, but I had also started to realize that it was time for me to grow up and that maybe she was the one I could grow up with. We shared some of the same challenges that came from being raised in predominantly black communities. Her parents liked me too, and it just seemed like we would be a good fit for each other. When I told her about my child and the circumstances with his mother, she had no problem with it. We were doing well as a couple, and I was actually starting to feel happy being with just one person for once in my life.

We dated for several months before we began making long term plans to get married. I couldn't afford an engagement ring, so when she agreed to marry me, I gave her my high school ring as a placeholder.

While she and I were dating and getting engaged, my relationship with my son and his mother was strained. To be fair, I was just going through the motions. I didn't want to see her or be a father to a son. My times with him were good, but I couldn't help but feel like I was with someone else's child. His mother solidified that sense by making sure I constantly felt guilty, which always led to me being ashamed of myself. It became a vicious cycle that I subjected myself to over and over again.

I could have walked away from both of them. No one would have said anything to me, at least legally, but I couldn't do that to an innocent child. So, I continued to pay child support and visit with him whenever his mother would allow it. I also began to pray for God to please help me take care of my responsibility to the child, and accept the consequences of my actions like a man!

That was the browbeating tone of my prayers because I was so tired of my own behavior.

Despite it all, I started to formally babysit my son on the weekends when I came home to Louisville—and quite unexpectedly, we began to bond as a father and son. There was one weekend where I had him all by myself as I stayed at my sister's home. He and I slept together in the bed, we went to church, and I took him with me to visit some of my buddies from high school. It was a great, and I came to cherish those weekends. Sadly, they were going to become much more the exception than the rule.

That was what was happening in my life when I was horrifically burned in January 1980 and ultimately broke up with the woman who I thought was going to become my wife. I think we both would have been settling for a lifelong friendship, instead of a forever love affair, if we had stayed together.

That spring, I moved out of my room in the barracks and into an off-post apartment with a soldier that served in my unit. He was white, three years older, and we both viewed the world very similarly. We didn't get why some folks didn't like others just because of where they grew up or the color of their skin. Ironically, his name was Tony, the same as my third grade classmate and friend whose parents banned me from seeing him.

I continued babysitting, often at my apartment near Ft. Knox. His mother trusted me to take her son away from Louisville for those weekends, but it was mostly because she was still hoping there could be some kind of relationship between us. As I recovered from my burns, I remained upset with her.

She refused to give me a copy of the child's birth certificate. She would not agree to see an attorney or go to court. She rejected any notion of a paternity test. There were times she wouldn't even let me see the boy when I was available to do so.

She kept me in limbo the entire time, and I couldn't understand why. To not know whether or not the child was mine, and to not have any legal rights, was my purgatory—and I became so tired of being her puppet on a string. I could have acted like the whole sordid affair had never happened with his mother, now my torturer. After all, there were many young men my age who got girls pregnant and never took care of their child, whether their name was on the birth certificate or not! Yet I wanted to be better than that. One of my high school teachers had once told me that I would not be like most of the other young men who came from my neighborhood. Those words stayed with me. So, I rose above my emotions and determined to try to do the right thing for both the little boy and my soul.

My relationship with my son's mother was still touch and go, and there was no rhyme or reason to her behavior, when I met Erica at the disco in June 1980. She and I had been speaking to one another for only a couple of weeks when I built up the nerve to drop the "I have a baby" bombshell on her. I was reluctant to tell Erica because I was convinced that she was the one I had been searching for. I'd finally found her, and I didn't think I could survive her rejecting me on account of my sins. I also had to tell Erica that I was on permanent change of station orders from the Army and would be assigned to Germany in early 1981.

> I rose above my emotions and determined to try to do the right thing.

It was a lot to lay on a teenage girl, but I knew I had to put all of my cards on the table if a life with her was going to work. I fervently asked God to please allow Erica to stay with me—even though I had a child out of wedlock, was morally corrupt, and hadn't been a very good soldier up to that point.

My sense of self-worth was about as low at it could get.

I visited Erica at her parent's home, and we went into her living room to sit alone on the couch. My heart was pounding so hard I thought it was going to burst right out of my chest. I looked straight into her beautiful eyes, and Erica later revealed that my expression was serious, as though something was wrong.

I told her everything.

Her face scrunched up with a curious look as I spoke and stayed that way when I was finished talking. After what seemed like an eternity, but was in actuality no more than several seconds, she smiled and said of my son, "I can't wait to meet him."

Wow! I thought. *She must be an angel from God to accept an underperforming soldier with a burned face, a child, and a rucksack full of other emotional baggage.*

There was no doubt that I had hit the jackpot with this kind and beautiful girl!

Erica was, and remains, the love of my life. How do I know this? Just one of the reasons is her loving acceptance—for our first date in late July 1980 included the presence of my son.

I picked Erica up at her house in my Camaro with my son in his carrier in the back seat. She looked amazing in the white, yellow, and light blue flowered sweater that I had recently bought for her, white pants, and black open toed sandals. Her long, black hair was smoothly combed and flowed down her back, ending just short of her waist. She had a radiant smile, and she smelled even better. Her lotion reminded me of a crisp, fresh field of strawberries.

The latter was especially helpful for me since the boy, who by then was almost two years old, had filled his diaper right before I left to get Erica and still retained a scent of his own. As I labored to get rid of the overflowing mess without dirtying myself in the process, the sticky tape designed to hold the fresh diaper shut tore right off. Of course, it was the last diaper I had, so in typical Eagle Scout style, I improvised. I took a piece of Army olive drab duct tape and used it to secure my son's wrapping around his waist. It was quite a sight to see, but it was the best field expedience method I could come up with in the moment to fix the issue.

Thankfully, the diaper stayed in place, and my son cooperated with no further gastronomical outbursts, as we picked up food at a McDonalds in Radcliff, a beautiful, small, but thriving town outside of Ft. Knox, before taking her over to my apartment. When we arrived, I noticed that my roommate's car wasn't there. I assumed Tony was still out grocery shopping, one of his Saturday duties for us. Erica and I walked in the front door and directly into the living room area, and I placed my son in his carrier by the couch in front of the television. Our apartment was spotless as usual. In general, Tony was much more of a clean freak than I was, though my assigned areas of the apartment (my room, the bathroom, and the living room) were kept as tidy as I could possibly get them.

I turned on one of the cartoon stations for my son's amusement, then Erica and I went into my bedroom immediately adjacent to the living room. We could see my son from where we were sitting, so as he watched TV and fiddled with his red pacifier, we lounged on the edge of the bed, ate our food, and talked before heading back into the living room. Erica had done a lot of babysitting when she was younger, so she was comfortable with him, and he responded well to her. She played with him a little bit for the next hour until Tony returned and briefly met Erica, and then we left, and I took her back home.

It may not sound like much, but it was the perfect, low key, "get to know you" kind of date that gave Erica an opportunity to learn more about me and my son. As she recalls the date, Erica said butterflies were fluttering in her stomach, but it was more out of excitement for seeing me again than about meeting the boy. She thought he was a little cutie pie with tiny curls and a big smile, and while she did laugh at the duct taped diaper, she found it was quite adorable and creative, something that only a soldier would do.

But another thought was lurking in her mind: an image of her parents' disappointed faces and the broken hearts they betrayed. I didn't know it then, but they were not at all pleased with her decision to date me because I was a soldier, and she was still in high school. Yet Erica said she was well aware that she was going against her parents' will. In hindsight, she recognizes that their feelings were completely understandable. She was just a senior, and they felt that my life decisions up to that point would have a negative, if not harmful, effect on her life.

She had always loved and highly respected her parents and their words of love and wisdom, and she never wanted to hurt them in any way. But her emerging independence as a teenager, with its typical struggle between being a good daughter and satisfying her own curiosities, overrode what they had taught and advised her. So did her feelings about me. We had fun together. Meeting my son was interesting, she said, but it was kind of a sidebar next to being with me.

Incredibly, Erica remembers that she sensed that I was a loving person and that I already really loved her. She *felt* it—and though she wasn't aware then that she was already in love with me, she believes now that she must've been if she was willing to defy her parents the way she did. As Erica puts it now, she was all in.

It might sound corny, but even then, Erica was beginning to heal my wounds caused by the lack of love I felt when I was growing up, and she helped me to start to find my faith. Erica also focused me to be all I could be as a soldier. In some ways, she was more military than I was. She regularly asked me about my goals and how I expected to reach them. She made sure I arrived on time for duties. Most of all, she made me think about things in ways I had not done before, and her love was all the motivation I needed to really start applying myself toward my potential just as I had as a Boy Scout.

It was clear that Erica was not a lazy person, but I could also see that she appreciated it when someone did something for her. She helped me feed my son and clean him up. She spoke very proper and had great manners. While we were eating, Erica shared that she had attended a private Catholic school for many years prior to her attending public high school. She expressed how much her parents loved her and how they wanted her to marry someone who would treat her right.

I knew after that date that Erica was everything I was hoping for. I was learning to trust my intuition, and it screamed that Erica was the one. I had never felt that way about any of the previous girls in my life. I wanted somebody, or they seemed to want somebody, and our paths collided. Yet when I met Erica, it was totally different.

She wanted to break away from her parents and be her own person, and I believe I brought that out of her in a positive way. I had all of these things going on in my life, yet she not only accepted me, but she enjoyed being with me. I was a young man who had needed—even craved—acceptance all of my life, and Erica was providing just that in a genuine and authentic way.

So, how did I persuade this modern-day Cleopatra to fall for me? I viewed winning Erica like it was a military mission, devising a strategic plan with objectives and action steps to first have Erica become my girlfriend and then, hopefully, my wife for life! Although I had many flaws as a 19-year-old about to turn 20, one positive trait I felt that I possessed in abundance was the ability to be persistent and consistent in my pursuit of a goal or an achievement. I knew how to exercise self-discipline toward accomplishing something—when I really wanted it. I just hadn't exercised that gift very much because I was so steeped in sin.

It was only after I met Erica that I became motivated about life in general and found my zeal for being as good a soldier as I was an Eagle Scout.

Erica was the one thing I had been missing in life—and I knew that she was the key to me becoming a better person.

Yet the road ahead that would lead me to becoming that better person still had some unexpected curves and detours to come.

Chapter 3

THE FLAWED MAN'S PLAN
GETS A PARTNER

I used all of my free time, funds, and brain power to win Erica
Pettigrew over to becoming Mrs. Erica Hobbs! I made sure I
looked my best whenever I was with her. I spared no expense on
her, though I had little to expend after using what I needed for
my living expenses and paying my child's mother. I tried to take
Erica out at least once a week, and I even went to Catholic Mass
with her and her family one Sunday. Her father seemed a little
impressed with that, and he even invited me over to their home
for lunch after the service.

I saw that as a minor victory in my efforts to win over Erica's family, so I found as many other reasons as I could to continue to come by Erica's home to show her, and them, that I
cared for Erica. I gave her rides home after her drill team prac-
tices, rehearsals with a community performing group called the
Hardin County Singers, or the area modeling events she was
involved in. I literally lost my breath at one of those when she
walked down the runway in a red kimono dress offset by matching chopstick hair pins. She was stunning!

It wasn't just her parents that I had to convince. She had extended family living with her at the time: two nieces and two nephews. The nieces were both under the age of ten, and they immediately took to me. The nephews, though, were closer to Erica's age, quite protective of their auntie and, therefore, quite hostile toward me. There was one instance that almost came to fisticuffs, and they were more than ready to take me on, the rogue bouncer from the disco. "Look," I told them, "I don't want to hurt you guys. I appreciate that you are trying to take up for your auntie, but I'll win you over. Just give me time." I was as respectful as I could be. I certainly didn't want anyone in Erica's family, especially her father, to think that I went around beating people up every time I had a disagreement with them.

I pulled out all the stops—but I quickly realized Erica was not terribly impressed with anything I bought her, anywhere I took her, or even with anything I did to try to win over her family. She only wanted me to be kind to her and honest with her. The latter was the challenge: I had a lot of baggage, and I didn't know if she could take it if I started to unpack it.

Could I share my true self with Erica without scaring her away?

I decided to take a big chance. Over several conversations, I incrementally told her about some of my personal failings and shared the emotional issues I had been carrying from my childhood. I detailed how I came into the world and was abandoned by my father. I told her more about my upbringing and my sometimes-fractured family relationships, and I revealed how I felt that I wasn't the best soldier I could be. I admitted to Erica that I had dated many girls in the past to try to fill the hole in my heart that needed acceptance and validation. The fact that I had a son out of wedlock was a big deal to her, as were my two serious relationships before her and several other sexual relationships before that.

We even discussed how I—we—were going to deal with my son. We talked about possibly adopting him someday and trying to do a better job of co-parenting with his difficult mother. It was important to Erica that I not drop out of my son's life just because we were together. Her family was huge. Erica was the eighth of nine children with a 20 year span between them all, and she was her daddy's baby girl. Her two protective nephews were more like brothers to her, and she went to the same high school as the oldest of them. Therefore, family was everything to Erica—and I wanted to do everything I could to honor that with her loved ones as well as my son.

To my surprise, Erica was still on board with our relationship. After all, she said she hadn't been perfect with all of her decision making, either, and told me that she respected me and fully supported me trying to take responsibility for my son. I was overjoyed and relieved—which prompted me to move forward with the next objective in my strategic plan.

Erica and I had been dating for about four months when I asked her to be my fiancé. It was during Thanksgiving weekend 1980. We spent the holiday together at her parent's home. By then they realized that I was serious about their daughter and had started treating me with a more welcoming attitude. In fact, I had actually talked to Erica's dad a few days earlier. He didn't pull any punches, telling me that he would allow me to marry Erica, but that he had two requirements before I could receive his permission to get married.

First, I would have to be promoted to sergeant. Second, Erica would have to finish high school.

The problem with his demands was that they meant I would have to move to Germany without yet being married to Erica, save enough money to fly back to Radcliff after she graduated from high school, and somehow achieve rank as a sergeant. "Sir," I replied politely, "I respect what you're asking me to do. You are asking me to go to Germany, go through the promotion system if they have a slot, go to school to make E-5, save money, fly back home to get your daughter, get married, then get us a home, secure her ID card and passport, and take her back to Germany?" I took a deep breath. "Sir, that is quite a bit."

I wondered if he realized it would take me at least three years to achieve E-5, or sergeant, rank. But I was thinking, *You are not going to tell me how to skin this cat.*

He was unmoved. "Those are my demands. Erica is still in high school. She is still a minor. You've got to respect that."

I did, to a point. Yet I was at the place, after seeing my own family's broken history, my history of almost getting married, and understanding that Erica's older sisters had similar situations that hadn't worked out, that come hell or high water, I was going to make it work with Erica. My attitude was, "Even if we fall out of love, what's love got to do with it? We'll fall back in love."

Erica's mind was made up, too. Her parents had set an example of a lifetime marriage, so she went into our relationship believing that it was going to be a lifetime thing. The opposition we were facing just gave her that much more incentive and determination to make sure our relationship would be forever. As far as her father's ultimatum was concerned, she believed that her parents hoped it would cause us to separate. They were hoping we would fall out of love. Her dad's demands, even if they had been realistic, meant she and I wouldn't be together for a long time. As she saw it, I'd have to do that tour in Germany all by myself. "If he still loves you when he comes back," they told her, "then you'll be fine."

I appreciated that her father's rigid requirements showed that he was thinking about his daughter's future, well-being, and safety—but they broke my heart and made me that much more determined.

The night before I asked Erica to be my fiancé, I prayed. "God, no matter how much I plan or how well I execute it, it will only work if I put it all in your hands." Although I still felt like I was living in sin, I somehow knew the Lord would hear the prayers of a repentant person who was trying to do better in life.

The next morning was Thanksgiving Day, and my stomach was swarming with a kaleidoscope of butterflies as I drove to Erica's home to have dinner with her and her family. Erica's mom was a great cook, and the meal—turkey and ham, cornbread stuffing, cranberry sauce, mashed potatoes and gravy, green beans, collard greens, and a bevy of different cakes and pies— was excellent, even if it did little to calm my nerves. After dinner, she and I were alone in the basement sitting on the couch. I looked into Erica's eyes.

"I know we have an incredible future together. I can't imagine living my life without you—and I love you so much. Will you marry me?"

She smiled, lighting up the room. "Yes!" she replied, then added, "I love you, too."

It was the first time she had said those words to me—and they changed my entire world. After a few near misses, I had gained my soulmate for life. I also knew, from then on, that I would continue to put my life's plans in God's hands. I felt like I was saved. That moment literally rescued my life.

For her part, Erica was excited, but she wasn't surprised. She later revealed that there was no doubt in her mind that she wanted to marry me despite how much she was going back and forth worrying about what her parents thought of us. She was surprised that they had asked me to join them for Thanksgiving, and she thought that was a big deal in and of itself. She was so thankful that we could be together in front of them and that all of her siblings and their families that could be there had that opportunity to get to know me better. Erica knew cooking was her mother's way of sharing love and bringing everyone together—and I was a part of it!

> After a few near misses, I had gained my soulmate for life.

Just in time, too. My departure for Germany was set for February 22, 1981, the clock was ticking, and I had no intention of leaving without Erica being my wife. Yet we didn't formally agree to get married prior to my departure for Germany until early February. We were at my apartment.

"I am so in love with you," I said, "that I cannot travel there without ensuring that you are my wife." I also told her that I did not want to wait for her parents. There was no way that I could meet her dad's requirements before I had to leave. On the more practical side, being married to Erica prior to my move to Germany would allow me to immediately start setting up her travel orders as my wife prior to her graduating high school.

Erica wanted to obey her parents. In retrospect, she believed that if I hadn't been scheduled to go to Germany, we would have been willing to wait to be wed. But she also knew I would be leaving soon, and she did not want to be without me. She was elated when she accepted my marriage proposal, and she wanted to be my wife. Yet she also wanted to graduate high school.

Time was running out. We needed hope and a plan, and between the two of us, we were determined to come up with one.

In many places throughout the Bible, we are told to honor our father and mother, and Proverbs 23:25 adds, "May your father and mother rejoice; may she who gave you birth be joyful!" Erica knew that she hadn't been raised to do some of the things that she was doing with me. She even found herself questioning who she was as a result of it all. At times, such quandaries overwhelmed her heart and mind, and she felt extremely disappointed in herself. She wavered between following her parent's instructions and accomplishing her own desire to be with me. Her battle was similar to how Paul must've felt in Romans 7:21-25 when he struggled with knowing that he should do one thing but ended up doing the opposite.

The struggle was real! Yet her love for me overshadowed everything.

In the midst of her inner turmoil, I thought about my own upbringing, and it made me want to be part of their family. At the same time, though, I viewed our situation as one of those small windows of opportunity in life that I couldn't allow to close without taking action. I was a military man. I knew I had the high ground, the strategic advantage, and I wasn't going to waste this moment on a "would've, could've, should've" scenario.

I also felt like I had to close the deal before Erica possibly came to her senses and realized what a risk it was to marry me and my rucksack full of problems. I genuinely feared that if Erica didn't marry me before I went to Germany, I would have been so dejected, hurt, and confused that I would have fallen back into trying to fill the emotional holes in my life with one bad relationship after another.

Erica was 17, and in Kentucky I knew we wouldn't be allowed to get married until her eighteenth birthday in June. But I had heard from someone that we could be wed before her birthday in Gallatin, Tennessee. I had no way to confirm that information back in those pre-internet days, but I felt it was our only chance before I had to go overseas, and I was willing to do whatever it took.

I was short on cash, so I pawned the high school ring that I had previously given to my first fiancé for gas money. Erica went to school that Friday morning and cut class after homeroom to meet me in the parking lot. We drove 127 miles to Gallatin. But when we got to the justice of the peace, we were told that the legal age of marriage had been moved forward. She had to be 18 in order for us to get married there.

Crushed and broke, we began the drive back to Radcliff. Erica started crying, and I sheepishly asked her what was wrong.

"I'm disgusted with myself for sneaking around, lying to my parents about where I am, and cutting school," she said. "I'm also feeling very guilty about having regular sex with you outside of marriage. That's not how I was raised, and I know God is not happy with me or you."

I was floored by her statements, but I also realized that Erica was right. I pulled the car over and we both wept and hugged one another. It was a defining moment that we will never forget.

But I remained too driven to stop. We *had* to be married before I went to Germany.

I looked at Erica, hoping she would automatically know the context of my question.

"Are you still with me?"

Determined to be with the man she loved, Erica nodded. "Yes, I am. When we get married, we can ask God and my parents to forgive us, and we will dedicate our lives to each other for life."

———————

I purchased a very small diamond ring for Erica after two months of saving up money instead of eating out, going to the movies, or any other non-essential purchases. I picked her up one day after school, and when she got in the car, I gave her the box with the ring. She opened it and gave me a big kiss. "This is all I can afford, but one day I will buy you the ring you want, and you'll never have to worry about being able to afford to pay your bills on time," I promised. I hoped she could see that I was becoming a man of my word who would fulfill his promises by making whatever sacrifices were needed.

Erica was excited but not totally surprised. I had promised her a diamond ring and a fur coat when we first started talking about getting married, so she knew it was coming. It seemed surreal, but it was really happening, and she said it just made her love me all the more.

The following weekend, Erica and I visited her sister and brother-in-law in Indianapolis, Indiana. I had just received my pay from the Army to fund the getaway, but I still promised myself that I'd return to the pawn shop and get my high school ring back—after I married Erica.

The trip was Erica's idea, and the plan was simple but devious enough. She took her birth certificate from where it was stored inside her mother's China cabinet. Her brother-in-law was an executive at a local company and had to go into the office that weekend to work. We'd go there, use his copier machine to copy the certificate, use correction fluid to white out her birth year of 1963, type in 1962, and then make another copy to create the forgery.

Her brother-in-law was more than willing to be our accomplice. He was one of our biggest supporters then and remains so to this day. He has been like a brother to me as well as a trusted mentor who was successful both in his corporate job and in the Army reserves. He is an example of success that I have followed throughout my adult life.

With the fake birth certificate secured and the original stealthily returned to the China cabinet, Erica cut school again that Monday morning, and we drove to the Elizabethtown, Kentucky Justice of the Peace with a crisp ten dollar bill in hand. Elizabethtown was only about 12 miles from Radcliff, so it was the most convenient place to try to see if our forged documents would work.

We did not miss Exit 60b, and when we arrived at the courthouse, we were met there by my best friend from high school. He was the same guy whose pay I had docked when I was a supervisor at the park. We'd actually known one another since grade school, and I rode to school with him every day since my junior year in high school in his cool yellow Chevy Camaro. He was set to be my best man. One of Erica's close friends, who she had sung with in high school choir and with the Hardin County Singers, also met us there to be her maid of honor. Forty years later, she'd tell Erica that she never told anyone about our elopement. Both friends served as witnesses.

After entering the office of the Justice of the Peace, I paid $5.00 for the judge to officiate the proceedings, and we were told by his secretary to please wait until he was ready. The room was small with a couple of chairs and pictures of previous justices of the peace on the wood paneled walls. I glanced around with excited anticipation, fearing that if the forged certificate was discovered, everything would come tumbling down.

A few minutes later, the judge called us back into his office. He had a huge desk of shellacked wood, and there was a little podium off to the side. I assumed that's where he would stand to marry us—if we got that far.

The judge asked us to sit down, and we handed him our birth certificates and the results of the state required blood tests that we had done at a free clinic two days earlier. If anyone there thought Erica might have been underage, no one said anything.

He looked everything over—and noticed right away that Erica's birth certificate was not the original. "Why have you brought a copy?" he asked.

We had already agreed to support each other's lies, and Erica was ready with a response. "My original birth certificate was burned in a fire," she stated confidently. "That's why this one is a copy."

The judge hesitated at first, but then he graciously accepted her explanation. It was plausible, all things considered, and it wasn't like he could go online back then to fact check her story. Erica didn't feel bad about lying to him, but she also didn't realize how serious a deception it was.

Neither did I. I just wanted to see it through.

The judge smiled. "So, are the two of you ready to get married?"

"Yes, sir!" the two of us declared simultaneously. I exulted inside. *This is really going to happen.* I thought to myself. *I can't wait!*

"Please stand up and follow me," he directed.

The judge guided us over toward the podium. As he took his place behind it, an unexpected thought crossed my mind.

Maybe, just maybe, God is proud of me for doing the right thing for once and is actually helping me make my plan come true.

I really felt like it was all in God's hands now.

The judge read the standard vows, and we repeated them to one another as required. Both of us said our "I do's" and the ceremony ended with his directive, "You may kiss the bride."

I looked into Erica's beautiful eyes and gave her a passionate kiss. It all happened so fast that it felt like I was having an out of body experience. Erica was excited with the realization that she was my wife and I was her husband!

We were Mr. and Mrs. Harry Hobbs!

We signed the certificate of marriage in the correct spots and left the judge's office. Our friends drove away, her friend back to school and my friend to his home, and Erica and I took the remaining $5.00 I had to buy a three-piece chicken meal from KFC. We split it in the car.

It was the best wedding reception ever!

It was also the happiest day of my life! I couldn't believe I had just married the woman of my dreams who said I was the man of *her* dreams! It felt just like one of those old movies I used to watch with Big Daddy in the basement where the leading man got the beautiful, leading lady.

> I couldn't believe I had just married the woman of my dreams.

Today, I often refer to my wife as my girlfriend because Erica was my last girlfriend, and it keeps us young thinking about those crazy early years together. We realize how far God has brought us and how we can now help others make better decisions. That's why we often provide pre-marital counseling to young couples (including telling them the story of our three-piece chicken meal), and I have officiated several marriages since becoming an ordained minister in 1992.

It wasn't until a few days after we were married that I looked at the marriage certificate and noticed that it indicated my ethnicity as white and Erica's as black. Talk about living in the middle of the color line. My birth certificate stated that I was black.

Not that being black or white mattered to me at that moment. My most important identity was set. I was Erica's husband! I was about to become even more than that.

That night, Erica's parents allowed me to spend the night in her room with the understanding that I would sleep on the floor while Erica slept in her bed with her big sister. They realized that Erica and I were about to be separated for a long time and that I had to leave early the next morning to drive all day to the military port in Charleston, South Carolina before departing for Germany on February 22.

Of course, what her parents didn't know was that we had been married that day and it was our wedding night—but Erica's sister, who was visiting from Indiana, did know, and she let Erica sleep beside me on the floor. She would've likely been too uncomfortable letting us share the bed.

We spent that first night as husband and wife snuggled together, sad and fully clothed, so it wasn't exactly the wedding night of our dreams. But it was more than enough for us, and I was grateful to Erica's sister for allowing us to sleep side by side.

I woke up early with Erica in my arms, and I immediately gave her a big kiss. For that brief moment we forgot that her sister was in the bed above our heads. We quietly ended our embrace, I went into the bathroom to get dressed, and then came out to say my goodbyes to Erica. I had to get on the road right away.

It was the hardest goodbye I'd ever had because, for the first time in my life, I was departing from someone who completely loved and accepted me. I understood that my family had loved me, too, but this was entirely different. I felt like I had been a problem for them, so when I left home to live on my own, I believed I was helping the situation by no longer hurting them. One reason I was so happy to join the Army was so I would be one less problem for my family to manage.

But I didn't see myself as a problem for Erica to deal with. It broke my heart to leave her.

It broke hers, too. She began to cry as I got in the car and put on my seatbelt. I had the window rolled down, and she leaned in and gave me a deep, passionate kiss.

"I love you," she repeated, "and I believe in your plan for our lives."

I headed toward the highway at 7:00 a.m., knowing that I would be staying the night in Charleston with Erica's sister's boyfriend. It was great to have his help, and I viewed it as another gift from God to make my journey away from the States, and from Erica, easier.

Throughout the 13-hour drive, I thought about how I was going to become a soldier any commander would be proud of, and one who was going to build a new life of fun, fellowship, and friendship with Erica founded on our unending love for each other. I concluded that we would always respect one another and work through our problems, no matter what life threw at us.

By the time I got to Charleston at 8:00 p.m., I was worn out. It was the longest time and distance that I had ever spent driving in my life. Erica's sister's boyfriend was great, and his mother was very kind to me. I learned that she had never spent time in her home with anyone who was biracial, and she made me feel so welcome. I had let my hair grow out full and curly, and his mother couldn't help running her hand through my hair and commenting how pretty and nice she thought it was.

I got up the next day and arrived at the military port, fed and well rested, by 8:00 a.m. sharp to drop off my car, a 1975 Pontiac Firebird I got in trade for my Camaro, prior to going to Germany so it could be shipped overseas. I then took a taxi to the Charleston Military Airlift Command to board the C-5 Galaxy transport aircraft for my flight, a 10-hour trek that crossed six time zones. It took off at high noon, and I couldn't help but feel like I was in an old western film playing the role of the lawman about to duel with the evil gunfighter. It was time for me to put up or shut up when it came to growing up and stepping up in a foreign country and becoming a real soldier!

I landed in Rhein-Main Air Base near Frankfurt, Germany around 5:00 a.m. local time, 10:00 p.m. United States Eastern Standard Time, so my body was ready for bed, not breakfast. Weary but excited, I was met by military representatives from the U.S. Army Seventh Corps after being assigned to one of the artillery units under its command. I stayed at Rhein-Main overnight at one of the transit barracks, giving me time to recover from an intense case of jet lag. As I reflected about Erica and being far away from her and from home for the first time in my life, I prayed. I asked God to help me become the best soldier I could be for my new wife and to empower me to get off on the right foot and impress my command by volunteering for every tough job and giving my full effort to be successful.

The next evening around dusk, I was picked up by my unit sergeant and four other soldiers and joined them on the journey to Herzo Base near Nuremberg, Germany three hours away. I rode with them in the back of a Gama Goat, a semi-amphibious off-road vehicle, with nothing more than my duffle bag packed with clothing and personal items. It was freezing cold, and as I watched the lush, green, hilly countryside go by, I thought to myself, *I am in the real Army now!*

Over the next six weeks, I settled in to my new reality in Germany and was forced to mature in ways I never had before. I had to get up on my own, clean my own room, do my own shopping and cooking, and give a full effort every day to be the best soldier in my unit. I was able to attend a four-week leadership course beginning the second week I was there. I graduated at the top of my class, earning soldier of the month and soldier of the quarter awards for my battalion in the process.

In no time flat, I succeeded in becoming one of the best members of my unit in the areas of drill and ceremony, physical training, land navigation, common task training, and military appearance—and it was all thanks to Erica. She became my source of motivation, my secret weapon to excel in the military. Marrying her caused me to become laser focused on being the best at whatever I needed to master in the Army. In Erica, God had truly given me the other piece I needed to succeed in life!

I began saving every extra penny beyond my living expenses toward a down payment on an economy apartment for us and Erica's ticket to Germany. The Army would've paid for her trip there and back, but only if we had agreed to stay in Germany for a three-year tour, commonly referred to as being command sponsored. But we chose to stay for just 18 months, agreeing that we didn't want to be away from our families back in the

States any longer than that. We were kids just trying to learn how to live on our own.

Back in the States, Erica was missing me so much that she had a hard time focusing on her schoolwork and often day-dreamed about being with me. Since we didn't have cell phones, internet, or any other mode of communication except writing letters in 1981, we wrote one another many times. Each letter took at least two weeks to arrive. Erica scented the paper and envelopes with her sweet perfume, and in one of my return letters I included a photo of me wearing my plain black Army physical training shirt and white painters' pants. She thought it was adorable and that I looked like a soft, fresh, cuddly teddy bear. It made her miss me all the more.

We could hardly wait until we could be together again, but we knew that wasn't going to be until after Erica graduated in late May. That's when we had planned for her to be able to leave the States to come live with me in Germany. Since we were mar-ried, we figured that her parents would have to let her leave then because she would be finished with school.

As far as we were concerned, everything was in place.

Then I got a letter from Erica with some unexpected news: she had missed her menstrual cycle. The obvious implications made me nervous, but I wasn't overly concerned because I had read somewhere that women sometimes miss a cycle when they are under stress—and Erica was under the most pressure she had ever experienced in her young life. Finishing school, going against her parents, being separated from me, and preparing to live in a foreign country was more than enough for a 17-year-old girl to manage. The cumulative effect of everything going on, and the emotions of having to deal with it all, must've been over-whelming. Stress made sense.

Then, in early April, Erica woke up one morning feeling nauseous, but she didn't get sick, and she felt better that evening. She assumed she had eaten something to upset her stomach or was perhaps fighting a virus.

Then it happened again and again—and her mother took notice.

"Oh, no!" she told Erica matter-of-factly. "I see that Harry left a package behind!"

Erica had also been having some strange dreams; specifically, of fish swimming in the water. "There's an old Philipino wives' tale," her mother told Erica. "If a woman dreams of fish swimming, then she must be pregnant."

The news left Erica shocked and speechless, but she figured that if anyone would know if she was pregnant, it was her mother who had nine children of her own.

Needless to say, her parents were heartbroken. They cried and prayed for Erica, and it hurt her to see them in such pain. Her mother didn't even speak to her for almost two weeks. Over time, though, they began to accept her status as, in their minds, an unwed mother-to-be. They forgave her and even began showing her how to take care of the baby during the pregnancy and after it was born. They started preparing themselves to support Erica with love and grace as an unmarried single parent.

Erica struggled with her own guilt over the pregnancy, and she was grateful that her parents were willing to walk with her through the consequences of what Erica saw as her sin. For me, I was more happy than anxious. I was saddened that the son I already had would probably never see the world or ever really get to know who I was then or, by God's grace, who I would become in the future. His mother had made it very difficult for me to see him before I departed for Germany, and my times with him had been sporadic and haphazard. I assumed my visits were going to come to a complete end with me now overseas. But that sorrow was offset by the fact that I was going to have a child with the woman of my dreams!

Still, Erica's pregnancy was a bit of a surprise. We thought we had been careful enough. I had always used a condom, and we had utilized the rhythm method to time our encounters, but it wasn't enough.

Oddly, Erica wasn't the one to tell me she was pregnant. Instead, it was my company commander. When he called me in to see him with no explanation, I was scared to death. I assumed I had done something wrong. In a way, then, I was relieved when he told me that he had received a letter from Erica's mother stating that I had gotten her daughter pregnant out of wedlock—and that I needed to get in some type of trouble for what I'd done.

"We are actually married," I told him, "but her mother and father don't know that yet. When they do, though, her mother will learn to love me for taking care of her daughter."

My reaction to him was needlessly defensive and really not much of a response at all, but it sounded good at the time and made me feel a bit less like a dirtbag. Erica's mom had every right to be upset with me. I had promised her and her husband that I wouldn't get Erica pregnant. Of course, that was nothing more than false bravado knowing we were having sex regularly.

Against her mother's hopes, my company commander was not upset with me at all. He did recommend that I should be more honest with people in my life going forward.

That evening, early morning back in the States, I called Erica on the ridiculously expensive German public phone system. She sounded very sleepy, but we nevertheless discussed how we would take care of our child. We also talked about her morning sickness and how tough it was for her being pregnant while in high school.

I was sympathetic—until she told me that a girl at her school had invited her to go to the prom. I went ballistic, telling her that was unacceptable and that she would be just fine missing her prom.

I reacted the way that I did because I knew that a boy who liked her, and who had even tried to date her while we were together, was going to be there. Erica insisted that she wasn't thinking at all about that guy. She simply wanted to go stag with her girlfriend—but I wouldn't stand for it, even adding that she wasn't the only one making sacrifices. In the end, Erica disagreed, but she respected my wishes and chose not to go.

> I should be more honest with people in my life going forward.

I was young and jealous, and in some ways, I regret that I took that experience away from her, but I know over the years I have more than made up for it.

We closed out the phone call agreeing that we would let her parents know that we were already married as soon as we felt the time was right, though we did not know yet exactly when that would be. I also reassured Erica that I was going to work hard to get promoted and that I was putting away money to pay for her to come to Germany after she graduated high school. She could have the baby in Germany, and we could start our life together as a family.

After ending the call, I walked around the artillery base for a while thinking about the future for me and my new family. Before going to sleep, I again prayed to God, this time to help us somehow make our big mess come out right for everyone involved. I pleaded with Him to cause me to grow up, be a man of my word, and take care of my wife and baby. I also prayed for my son's mom to allow me to do whatever I could for him.

It was at that moment in my life that I promised God and myself that I would become one of the best soldiers in the history of the U.S. Army. I had said that before, and I realize that such audacity sounds self-aggrandizing, but I have learned that when you have the right motivation in life, and God on your side, anything, and I mean *anything*, is possible! As Jeremiah 29:11 declares for all of us, "I know the plans I have for you ... plans to prosper you and not to harm you, plans to give you hope and a future."

I went to bed that night with an assurance from God that I would somehow survive my many mistakes in life and find a way to succeed as soldier, husband, father, and most importantly, as a Christian—as long as I eventually took the final step of giving my life to Christ, instead of being someone who was only an occasional visitor to God's throne, and who only asked for His help when I needed it.

That was going to prove to be much harder than I thought.

Chapter 4

THE FLAWS IN THE PLAN
START TO MANIFEST

Beware of family bowling night.

By May 1981, Erica was four months pregnant. She had begun feeling tired most of the time, especially at school. She hadn't informed her teachers or anyone else except her closest friends that she was going to have a baby. Somehow, her English teacher knew and was very sad for Erica, but showed her much grace during class, giving Erica lots of hugs and ample time to complete her work. Erica could feel her love and concern, and she really believed her teacher was praying for her and her family.

With that as the backdrop, Erica did her best to muscle through a regular family outing that she usually enjoyed: bowling night. It was at what is now the well-known Houston Bowling Center in Ft. Knox, and many friends and family joined them each time to bowl together. In attendance on this particular night was the mother of one of Erica's friends who knew she was pregnant.

Erica waved at her on the way to one of her more frequent visits to the restroom. When Erica returned, she immediately noticed that her mother looked upset. More than that, she appeared to be heartbroken and flushed with humiliation.

She pulled Erica aside where no one could overhear her. "How could you embarrass me like that?" her mother asked sternly, but not too loud. "Your friend's mother congratulated me on your marriage to Harry! I was speechless and had no idea what she was talking about. She read about it in the newspaper!"

Erica and I had no clue that all marriage license notices were published in the local newspaper.

Erica just stood there dumbfounded and guilt-ridden. Once again, she had hurt her parents to the core, perhaps even deeper this time. It felt to Erica as if she had just sliced their hearts in half and stomped on them. Her deceit continued to be revealed as if it were the midday sun shining on her life, and all of her selfish decisions were being fully exposed.

Her mother wept that night. So did Erica. Faraway in Germany, I was powerless to do anything about it. I can only imagine how hard that must've been for her.

A few days later, her parents let her know that they had extremely mixed feelings toward her. They felt some relief that she was not an unwed teenage mother who would have to rely on them to help her birth and raise the baby. I thought maybe her mother in particular would be at least happy with me about that, but she was even more angry with me. Again, she had every right to be, but I was truly convinced that, over time and with the help of the Lord, I would win her over and show her that I loved Erica and would take good care of her.

A week or so after the revelation at the bowling alley, we confirmed that Erica would be leaving for Germany quickly, the day after she graduated. Her parents were sad but not surprised to learn it was happening so fast. They were a close family, and the thought of having their youngest daughter taken away from them was devastating. Even though they felt that way, they knew it was best for everyone under the circumstances—and as much as Erica loved being with her parents and her family, she wanted to be with me more.

My brother, the one who was stationed with me in Germany, was scheduled to go on annual leave to Kentucky at about the same time Erica was going to graduate. He and I were still having some ups and downs in our relationship, even as adult soldiers living near each other, but we were growing closer every day, understanding that we needed each other more than ever. We were still maturing, trying to become better brothers and find true faith in God.

So, I asked my brother to help Erica get her military identification card and passport while he was home, and he graciously agreed. Erica's parents allowed her to take time off from school to go with him, a person she had never met before, to get the items she needed to be able to fly to Germany. My brother never charged me or Erica for anything. He had to drive 45 minutes south from Louisville to Radcliff to pick her up, take her to Ft. Knox to apply for and obtain the ID card, go back up to Louisville to apply for her passport, and then drive back to Radcliff to return her home before going back to Louisville to visit his friends and family. He even bought Erica lunch while he drove her around.

I respected my brother so much for his aid—and we will be forever grateful to him. Erica had no idea how to begin to accomplish those needs nor did she have the means to do so. My brother literally walked her through the whole process. Although Erica didn't feel at the time like she deserved such help, so strong was her guilt, he was such a Godsend to her that day.

That would turn out to be the first of many times my brother would step in to help me and my young family navigate life in Germany. As far as I was concerned, it was another miracle from God that hammered home the truth of Hebrews 13:1-2, which says, "Keep loving one another as brothers and sisters. Do not forget to show hospitality to strangers, for by so doing some people have shown hospitality to angels without knowing it."

Erica's graduation day for the North Hardin High School class of 1981 was truly one of great elation for her. She had anticipated everyone tossing their caps into the air to celebrate the culmination of their hard work. All of her family was there with their smiles and hugs! But the joyous occasion was more than a little bittersweet for her knowing that she was leaving the very next day.

Her entire family stayed overnight and went with her to the airport, showering her with love, prayers, and gifts: a wonderful Polaroid camera with extra film from her oldest sister who lived in Cleveland, and six crisp 20-dollar bills from her second oldest sister who lived in Chicago. That sister, who was like a second mom to Erica, started with one twenty and kept stuffing them into her hand, a tangible indication of just how worried she was about her little sister's upcoming travel and new life in Germany. Little did those two sisters know then just how much their gifts would mean to us.

Prior to going to the airport, the sister from Chicago had also taken Erica shopping for maternity clothes. Because she wasn't showing yet, everything was still too big for Erica. They picked out several two-piece maternity outfits with short-sleeved tops and matching jeans or shorts that had elastic front panels. Erica's favorite outfit had a casual white top with short blue sleeves and an adorable "Baby on Board" graphic with an arrow pointing down the front. The jeans were still so loose they often slipped off her waist, but that was the outfit Erica chose to wear on the plane. She also had a soft gray and white rabbit fur coat that I bought and sent to her so she could take it on board with her.

After arriving at John F. Kennedy International Airport in Queens, New York for her connecting flight overseas, Erica was so afraid and nervous about where to go to catch the second flight that she ended up riding the bus in a circle around the airport until it finally dawned on her that the gate for the connecting flight was literally right next door to the one where she had just gotten off. Erica's father had been a military man and her family was accustomed to traveling, so Erica was no stranger to flying. She was just distracted by her excitement of being on her way to see her beloved. During her nine hours in the air, Erica's joy was seasoned with moments of sorrow about being so far away from her family. She'd look out the window of the airplane, her vision often blurred by her tears, and watch the daylight change to dusk and back again as she crossed time zones.

Anticipating Erica's arrival, I had prepared everything we needed to successfully live in the economy apartment I procured for us off base. I had bought groceries and furnishings, found the books necessary to prepare her to pass the difficult German driving test, planned our hospital route and bus transportation to the U.S. Army Hospital in Nuremberg for maternity appointments, and had traded our U.S. dollars for deutschmarks at the bank.

We had been separated for just over three months when Erica finally landed in Germany weary with jet lag. The butterflies (and the baby) in Erica's stomach were fluttering as she disembarked, and she instantly noticed the temperature change from warm Kentucky to cold Bavaria. That fur coat came in handy to keep her warm over her thin short-sleeved maternity outfit. Her feet, clad in sandals, were still chilly. Yet when her gaze met mine, any discomforts were swept away as we ran into each other's arms.

The next few days were total bliss filled with hugs, kisses, catching up, and adjusting to our new life as husband and wife in the military. I showed Erica how and where to shop for our groceries and trade currency, and I introduced her to the leadership in my unit and their spouses. Erica and I had about 30 days to help her feel as comfortable as possible before I had to go on my first training exercise with my field artillery unit.

From then on, I was usually away, and I quickly realized that if I stayed in field artillery, I was going to spend most of my time apart from Erica, training in the beautiful but rugged countryside. I was gone every other month for about four weeks at a time. That, along with pulling overnight duty and going to classes, made things hard on Erica. Even though she was in Germany with me, Erica experienced true loneliness for the first time in her life. It had started for her back at home while I was away, and now the guilt she carried over from everything that had happened with her parents continued eating away at her. She couldn't help but feel like she somehow deserved the pain she felt, thinking that she had made her bed and now she had to lie in it.

Erica desperately missed her family, and my being gone so long on military duties didn't help. The sweet, lovely little "attic type" apartment I had prepared for us was fully stocked and very clean, but it was our first home as a couple, and it was one where Erica thought we'd be together most of the time. She'd always had family around her, with all the jabbering and noise that goes with it, and the apartment was too quiet. In addition, she was suddenly isolated in a foreign country and in a neighborhood off base where no one spoke English and she couldn't speak German. Every now and then, my leadership and their spouses checked in on her to make sure she was okay, and Erica never wanted them to leave. More than anything, she was afraid, particularly at night. Erica usually comforted herself by praying with the lights on until she fell asleep. Although she wasn't yet a Christian, Erica knew that prayer helped her feel better when she was sad or afraid.

We did the best we could as a husband and wife trying to make it in a foreign country. Whenever I was home, Erica curled up next to me in our bed to fall asleep with her head on my chest, listening to my heartbeat as I embraced her. There were days, due to our lack of income, when we just didn't have enough money to buy the food we liked or go to a movie, but I was always comforted by the thought that I was married to a wonderful young woman who loved me and would help me become the hero and leader I wanted to be. I kept reminding myself, *We are building a new life of fun, fellowship, and friendship. Our unending love will carry us through. We will always respect one another and work through our problems, no matter what.*

> Erica desperately missed her family, and my being gone so long on military duties didn't help.

Over the next few months, Erica and I observed the miracle of a growing child in her belly. The baby loved to kick and squirm, especially at night. I often talked to our baby as I rubbed and kissed her tummy. It was such a beautiful and amazing experience, and the child's presence brought peace and companionship to Erica when I was gone.

When Erica was seven months along, I took my Firebird to a person who worked at an auto and craft shop on base and did body work on the side. I'd had a minor fender bender before I left the States and believed I could get the repairs done before the baby was born. I turned my car over to him, along with five hundred dollars up front, to fix the damages.

Unfortunately, the person kept the vehicle for almost two months and did very little work on it. I wanted to beat him up for stringing me along and making me think that he would repair the Firebird. All he did was take our money, prep the vehicle for body work, and park the car in the garage. Exposed to the elements, the Firebird's body began to rust anywhere the metal was sanded or stripped.

I was so embarrassed about trusting him and displaying my poor decision making skills that I wallowed in self-blame. I didn't want to complain to my leadership about him cheating me because it was my fault to begin with. Sure, the guy later gave us an expensive camera to compensate us, and we took some wonderful photos before selling it for a couple hundred dollars. Nevertheless, my lapse in judgment caused us to be without our own transportation as the weeks counted down toward our child's due date.

On top of that, the Herzo Base flag football team, for which I played strong safety, were in the playoffs competing for the German military base flag football championship. There I was, traveling around Europe on the weekends to play football and dragging my wife along with me in the final weeks of her pregnancy. Erica was very understanding. She understood what a privilege it was for me to be a player on our team. My participation even allowed me to not have to go on field training exercises, so I could stay home and compete after we won the community and regional championships. In the end, we lost in the championship game, but I averaged one interception per game. It was just the start of Erica's unceasing support for me as an athlete in the Army.

With my Firebird temporarily out of commission, my brother helped us out once more by allowing us to occasionally borrow his second car, a used but workable Ford sedan, to get around in for the games and everything else we needed to do. We walked, got rides from friends, and took cabs to get places when we didn't have his car.

Erica's due date wasn't until November, but she ended up going into labor two weeks early—and in a rather unexpected fashion. On October 27, in my brother's Ford, we decided to head from our apartment outside Herzo Base to the hospital in Nuremberg as a test run for the real thing. Erica wasn't feeling well. She had been washing clothes at the laundromat, her stomach was nauseous.

She didn't know that she may have been having contractions. She wasn't in pain, but she could tell something was not right.

When we arrived, we told the nurses we were doing a practice run. They asked Erica some questions, and she informed them about the butterflies in her stomach. They checked her out.

"You are already dilated about four centimeters," the nurse said.

That scared us. We had no idea. Erica didn't feel she was ready to have the baby yet, but we were informed that she needed to stay at the hospital.

Erica was taken into a delivery room.

She delivered the baby an hour and a half later.

Everything happened so fast. Her discomfort quickly went from little twinges to excruciating pain. It was overwhelming for Erica. No one had told her it would hurt so bad, so she didn't understand how much anguish she would endure. She honestly thought she was going to die.

At one point, Erica twisted sideways, the instrument monitoring the baby's pulse fell off, and we couldn't hear the heartbeat.

I panicked. In that moment, I was convinced that *I* was being punished for my wanton fornication with Erica before we were married. Remembering the Bible stories I'd learned as a kid, my mind intuitively raced to the story of David and Bathsheba in 2 Samuel chapters 11-12.

We're going to lose our first child because of my sin!

Deathly afraid, I went behind the curtain next to her bed to pray.

Erica didn't know I had done that, and why, until decades later.

Of course, the sensor on Erica's abdomen was quickly replaced, and the sound of the baby's heartbeat returned strong and steady. I was then similar to the man behind the curtain in the Wizard of Oz. I was certain God was giving me a second chance—with all the brains, heart, and courage He could give me.

Next thing we knew, the infant's head was crowning. I held Erica's hand the whole time.

When the baby was born, Erica was in so much pain she couldn't even open her eyes after squeezing her eyelids shut so long from the strain.

But we had a girl. A lovely daughter.

A male nurse practitioner, a large fella that I estimate was about six-foot-six, took the baby to clean her up. He was moving around with her cupped in one, big paw of a hand, and I thought he was handling her roughly.

"Hey! You need to be more careful with my daughter and give her to me!" I hollered.

The emotion of the past several moments had gotten the better of me, but he was so kind. "Yes, sir," he replied gently. "I just need to clear her nose, and then I'm gonna give her to you." As he handed her over, I repeated needlessly, "That's my child. Be more careful!"

Then I hugged her and kissed her—and relief flooded my mind and soul. *Maybe I will have a chance to move beyond my past.* I thought as I looked into her little brown eyes. *My actions have had consequences that have changed me forever, hopefully for the good.*

I prayed to God to help me be a better father this time around.

Our daughter was nearly six-and-a-half pounds, 18 inches long, and healthy when she was born in October 1981. She was great company for Erica when I was away, and she provided Erica with the opportunity to nurture her and learn, by trial and error, how to properly take care of a newborn. Erica often wished she had her mother available to talk to and show her how to do just that. Unfortunately, the Army had very few resources to help new mothers. Occasionally, Erica asked other military moms how to do certain things, but they were not much older or any more experienced than she was.

So, Erica generally figured things out for herself. She had done a lot of babysitting as a teen, but those kids had been older, not infants. Yet she managed, often getting lost in the wonder of our daughter's tiny little hands and feet. Erica would spend hours just staring at the baby as she hugged her, fed her, changed her, and loved her. It was a time of discovery only a mother can truly understand.

I'll always remember one Saturday morning when I was taking care of our baby girl while Erica was cooking in the kitchen. I held her in my arms and kissed her jaws as she looked up at me with a big smile that made me feel like I could overcome my failures, beat the odds, and become a better father, husband, and soldier. Nearly my entire family came from broken homes. Almost every adult was divorced or remarried. I looked into my daughter's eyes and pledged to her that Erica and I would stay together and that we would always love her, come hell or high water!

We finally got the Firebird back, unrepaired, from the shyster who had promised to work on it. It wouldn't get fully fixed until we returned to the States after that first tour of duty. In the meantime, we began using the Polaroid camera from Erica's sister to capture the first of many wonderful moments together as a family. I took it to take pictures of me during field training exercises, and that initial $120 from her other sister certainly helped us as well.

Our baby was about six months old when our young marriage received its first test from outside influences; specifically, a soldier in my unit who tried to flirt with my wife. A few months later, the wife of another soldier in my unit attempted the same stuff with me. Erica and I didn't even realize it was happening at first. After those incidents, Erica and I both realized that we had to be careful with how friendly we were with others to ensure we weren't sending out any subconscious message that we were open to extramarital relationships. We tried to be nice to people, and we smiled a lot. We were pretty naïve, being as young as we were and living in a foreign country. All we wanted to do was make some friends.

It is always a little flattering when someone flirts with you, but it can be dangerous to your marriage if you allow it to continue. Before you know it, you may encourage someone to pursue you romantically without even knowing you did. All men and women should take heed of the words from Matthew 19:6, which says of married couples, "They are no longer two, but one flesh. Therefore what God has joined together, let no man separate." The grass may seem greener on the other side, but you have no idea about the weeds you may encounter. Therefore, take care of your own yard, and it will be greener than you could ever have hoped for. As 1 Corinthians 13:7-8 states, love "always protects, always trusts, always hopes, always perseveres. Love never fails."

In April 1982, I was able to reenlist for a new military occupational skill prior to my permanent change of station move back to the United States. Erica and I agreed that I should get out of field artillery so we could spend more time together as a family. I wanted an MOS that would challenge me intellectually, provide a technical skill set that I could utilize in the civilian workplace someday, and allow me to not have to go on as many training exercises. My recruiter at Herzo Base found an opening for me as a missile systems repair technician. That MOS was taught at the Redstone Arsenal U.S. Army post in Huntsville.

Arrangements were made for me to end my tour in Germany. I paid for Erica and the baby to fly back to the States in May so she could visit her parents and family in Kentucky before I arrived in June to pick them up to move to Huntsville. My first tour was supposed to last 18 months, but it was decreased by two months so that I could start the next available technician course on time.

When Erica and I learned that we were going to live in Alabama, I was excited for the opportunity to learn a new MOS there, but we were immediately concerned. We recalled the state's flawed civil rights history, the past events in Birmingham, Montgomery, and elsewhere, and were more than aware that Alabama was a notoriously racist part of the country. As it was, many blacks often thought I was white. Many whites believed Erica was black. So, as a half-black, half-white man with a brown girl who had already experienced her share of prejudice growing up in Kentucky, we prepared ourselves. To some in Alabama, we were a fatal hookup. We weren't supposed to be a couple, much less married and with a daughter.

The color line in America was real—and we were going to be straddling it like never before.

It had only been a month, but I was so excited to see Erica and our daughter when I got back to the U.S. Just as I'd hoped, Erica's parents had forgiven me and accepted us. They saw that I was taking good care of their daughter and granddaughter, and they were very kind to me. We also visited my family in Louisville while I was on travel leave. They saw that I had learned to pay my bills, take care of myself, and be a leader in the Army just like I was in the Boy Scouts.

> When Erica and I learned that we were going to live in Alabama, we were immediately concerned.

My mother, Big Mama, Big Daddy, and my aunt were all very happy for me. I wanted my family to see that they made the right choice by letting me live—not so much to impress them, but by doing my fair share, earning my keep, and showing that I was all the characteristics I'd learned as an

Eagle Scout: trustworthy, loyal, helpful, friendly, courteous, kind, obedient, cheerful, thrifty, brave, clean, and reverent.

Both of our families could see that we were more mature and responsible since going to Germany, and they were proud of us for making it through that time together and for taking such good care of our baby. We weren't the best parents in the world, but we did the best we could. Our daughter was always fed, clean, and well dressed. Her hair was always brushed, and we often received compliments about how cute she was. We were inexperienced as parents, but we were growing, and it showed.

We also went to visit my son, who was almost four years old, so he could meet his sister. I picked him up and gave him a big hug, and he was so happy to see me and his new extended family. But I noticed he had trouble fully stretching out his left arm, and his left leg didn't seem to be as strong and developed as his right one. His mother confirmed that the conditions were the result of his difficult birth, adding that he would be going to physical therapy to try to get as much movement and growth as he could on the left side of his body.

I was overcome with guilt and sorrow for my son's medical condition. I couldn't help thinking that it was just another consequence of my sins now being passed on to others, in this case, an innocent child. I was determined to be in my son's life and help him in any way I could, but his mother continued to make it hard for Erica and me to see him or allow him to go places with us.

As I watched my son and his sister play together on the floor, what I already knew from the Word of God was confirmed: it was not God's plan for a father to have children with different women and then try to patch together some semblance of a family. I had placed myself, my wife, my son's mother, and these innocent children in an emotionally difficult situation.

Little did I know then that I would spend the next 37 years trying to make my family situation work while treating my children as equally as possible, even while they lived in separate homes, using the love and resources God had provided me. I did the best I could with them over the years until tragedy struck my son later in life.

When we arrived at Redstone Arsenal, we went to the office to sign up for government housing on the post, only to discover that there were no units available for us. We had no other choice than to live off post, and the only places we could afford were lower income options.

I blamed myself, and I was upset that I had to make that type of housing choice with my young wife and newborn. I wished I had somehow been wiser with our limited resources. I had not only used our funds to make sure Erica and the baby could return home when they did without command sponsorship, but we had also sent money home to both my son's mother and to Erica's family to help with other needs and provide funds for them to buy things like groceries and baby items while Erica and our daughter stayed with them before my return.

I was so ashamed. Erica says I always felt like I had to prove myself to my family and hers—and she's right. I carried that responsibility like a lead weight. As we selected our small, studio apartment in a rundown complex we could barely afford, it only made that burden heavier.

We moved into the apartment early in the morning, and we couldn't help but notice that the other all-white families around us were none too pleased to see us. We shrugged it off as just being paranoid, but that first night affirmed our worst fears. It started around 10:00 p.m. with a knock on the door. When we answered, no one was there. It happened again and again, and we soon realized that we were being harassed. Troubled and afraid, we made it through the night.

The next morning, I left to head off to my first day of missile technician training—only to find that one of my tires had been slashed and that the gas cap on the side of the car was open. Glistening white powder was spilling over onto the pavement. A quick check confirmed that sugar had been poured into my tank.

I went back into the apartment to let Erica know what had happened and that I had called the police. When the officer, a white man, arrived, he inspected my vehicle and walked around the complex with a huge frown on his face. I was standing in the parking lot when he returned. "Could you please get your wife? I need to talk with both of you."

She came down, our daughter in her arms, and he gave us the harsh news. "Y'all are a mixed couple and are living in the wrong neighborhood for your kind. That don't go over well here," he said, punctuating the words with his thick southern accent. "Did y'all know a prostitute used to live in that there apartment? Because of that, summa the folks here probably thought your wife was a prostitute with you."

I was upset enough when he added, "Boy, you could've prevented this had you known where you were living to begin with. If I was you, I'd move my family to another part of town."

I took a deep breath and tried to reason with the officer. "We are both human beings. We should not be persecuted, vandalized, and bullied just because of the color of our skin. We don't even know anyone here. This is our first full day in Huntsville."

He just nodded his head. "You should get with your landlord and request to move to a neighborhood that will better accept your kind."

I couldn't believe it. Even he made the same wrong assumptions about our races, just like everyone else did.

The officer filled out a report, but I could tell he had no intention of conducting an investigation to find the culprit or culprits responsible for terrorizing me and my young family. I contacted my training unit, told them that my vehicle had been vandalized, and let them know that I had to get the repairs done before I could come in. My new commander was very kind and encouraged me to take my time to see to my vehicle and make sure my family was okay. The Army was good at allowing soldiers to take care of their problems and families as long as they gave their all when on duty.

I called a garage to come pick up my car, drain the tank, and replace the damaged tire. I arrived at my first day of training by 2:00 p.m. and had to play catch up the next two weeks to get back on track with my fellow technicians.

Welcome to Alabama.

To his credit, the landlord helped us relocate two days later to another one of his apartment complexes in a safer part of town about a mile away, even if the apartment itself was no better quality than the first. Thankfully, that was the last of any overt racial aggression toward us—and it would be nearly three decades later that I became a spokesperson for the Huntsville Police Department in 2010 and shared that story with the chief of police who hired me. He told me to let him know if I ever came across the officer who responded to us that day so that he could ensure he had become a better officer than he was in 1982, but I never saw him during my time with the department.

My missile systems repair technician training took six months, was enjoyable, and built my self-confidence. It was during that training that I met Greg, the instructor and Baptist minister who came to our apartment, spoke to us about the story of Joseph, and led me in a prayer to ask Jesus to forgive me of my sins and come into my life.

From that moment on, I became a Christian. It was the harvest from all of the seeds of faith that had been sown into my heart since I was a small boy. I still carried a truckload of guilt and shame that needed to be dealt with, and it would lead to ups and downs along the way as I progressed into a fully mature Christian, but at least I had a place to start.

I visited my son in Louisville several times during those six months. He and my daughter became very close in that short period, and my son's mother relented a bit, allowing Erica and I to spend more time than I expected with him so that we could all bond with each other. He was a very bright child, and he had a vivid imagination, too. He could create just about anything with his plastic building bricks, and he also loved playing video games. He was the life of the party when we visited him, and Erica and I enjoyed several family outings to amusement parks and movies with my son and our daughter.

> From that moment on, I became a Christian.

It looked as though a healthier co-parenting process might be possible. At the same time, though, my son's physical disability stemming from his birth began to be more noticeable. He was slightly paralyzed on his left side, and his arm and leg on that side were a bit smaller than his other arm and leg.

A couple of months before I graduated from my training, Erica and I were able to secure housing on post in a brick duplex with two bedrooms, one bathroom, and a small combo living/dining area. A sliding door off the kitchen led into a little backyard. All of the units looked the same, but they were clean and well maintained. We lived on Nike Street, a name that had nothing to do with the shoe, but the first nationwide air defense system dating back to the 1950s.

Meanwhile, near the close of my training, my oldest brother and sister informed me that my momma, who had been released from the mental health facility and had been staying with them at each one of their homes, needed a place to live. They were worn out from caring for her and dealing with her outpatient treatment regimen. They also said momma was getting emotionally out of control because she wouldn't take her medicine and became very agitated and aggressive as a result. Erica and I had never before observed these behaviors from her.

They asked me if we could take her in. We prayed about it and agreed to give it a go—even though I had just received my new orders to go to Ft. Riley, Kansas. We knew we were probably getting in over our heads, and it was a lot to ask Erica to allow my mentally ill mother to live with us and our little girl. We also decided to forego the arduous and time consuming process necessary through Army regulations to qualify momma as our official dependent, and that was a significant risk. If it was ever revealed that she was living with us and not just visiting, the consequences to my career could be severe. I was rolling the dice, yet I felt it was time for me to step up and give my siblings a break. I also wanted to at least try to give momma another chance to live a normal life, thinking back to how hard she had attempted to do the same for me during that short stint that my brother and I lived with her before our home burned down.

I suggested to Erica that momma could watch our daughter if Erica decided she wanted to find employment. Momma moved in with us a few weeks before I graduated from my training, and it wasn't long before we experienced our first challenge taking care of someone with mental illness. Momma had a schizophrenic episode in which she decided to call the military police in the middle of the night while Erica and I were asleep. She was convinced that someone had broken into our home and tried to attack her.

They arrived quietly, and it wasn't until Erica came awake and heard men talking with momma in the other room that she woke me up. We went in to see what was happening. The military police had assessed the situation and chosen to send her in via ambulance for a psychiatric evaluation.

Momma was admitted, but when we asked them to release her back into our custody, we were told they could not do so legally because momma was not our official dependent.

"Please release her," I pleaded. "I am a soldier, and I am being reassigned soon to Ft. Riley in Kansas. My mother needs to travel there with us."

The doctor relented and she was released, but only after I had pledged to get her mental health care when we arrived at Ft. Riley. The whole ordeal really threw Erica and I for a loop.

With that situation settled, we got ready for our move. I was so excited because I was assigned to the famous Big Red One First Infantry Division, the oldest, continuously serving division in the history of the U.S. Army. I was going to be the section chief for the tube-launched, optically tracked, wireless guided

(TOW) Dragon missile, one of the most technically demanding enlisted positions in the Army.

I was confident that my faith in God would enable me to overcome any and all fiery darts that the devil could throw at me (Ephesians 6:16).

But I'd soon realize that I had a lot more growing to do as we encountered a whole new set of challenges.

From 1947, a picture of my momma (left) and my aunt.

Still in my pajamas, I was ready to salute as I joined my family outside our
Louisville home in 1966. I was six years old.

At age seven, sharply dressed and saluting with my brother, who was two years older than me, and four of my cousins outside our home, 1967.

With my brother, who was two years older than me, smiling for the camera. He had cool suspenders!

Alongside the mayor of
Glenville, Kentucky as
the first Eagle Scout of
color in Troop 24, 1977.

With my baby son,
January 1979.

The day after being released from the burn
unit at Ft. Drum, February 1980.

With Erica in our first photo together, August 1980.

With Erica after I reenlisted in the U.S. Army at Herzo Base, Germany, Spring 1982.

Forty years later, with Erica after being inducted into the Warrant Officer Hall of Fame Eagle Rising Society at Ft. Rucker, Summer 2022.

With Big Mama at church after I completed
my first tour of duty, 1982.

With my oldest daughter in Huntsville,
Summer 1982.

Erica and I at our church
wedding, 1985.

During Operation Desert Storm testing a Bradley fighting vehicle during our area support missions, February 1991.

The burning oil wells during Desert Storm, February 1991.

Combat as it happened during the Gulf War, February 1991.

Feeding displaced Iraqi children during the ground war phase
of Desert Storm.

With my girls in Germany after
returning from the Gulf War,
Spring 1992.

With my daughters when I began to
experience PTSD, Fall 1992.

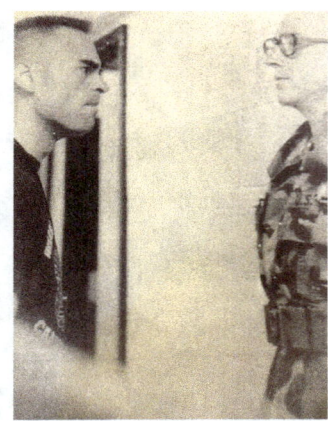

Showing that razor's edge as
I'm photographed as a TAC
officer giving directions to a
candidate, 1993.

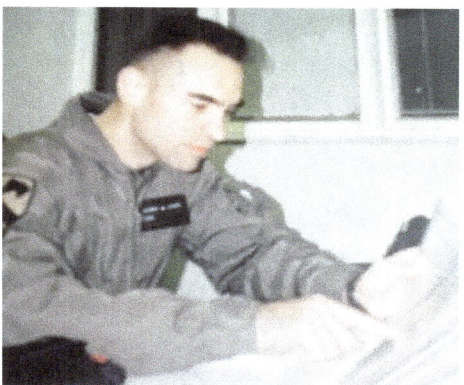

Prepping a flight plan before a
helicopter ride in 1993.

Preparing to jump with the famous
Golden Knights, 2013.

One of my favorite quotes and life principles
on the hallowed walls of the United States
Air Force Academy, 2014.

With Erica as a guest speaker at the ROTC Ball at
Alabama A&M University, 2016.

Speaking to JROTC
students in 2016.

At a high school reunion with, L to R, my
brother, who was two years older than me,
and my high school principal,
Summer 2022.

At Disney World with Erica
with our three youngest
grandchildren, 2022.

Erica and I with our bonus mom
and dad at a Korean War Veterans
celebration at Redstone Arsenal,
June 2022.

Receiving a community
leadership award from The
National Organization of Black
Law Enforcement in 2023.

Proudly wearing my ribbons at
a U.S. Army parade.

A moment of
forgiveness with my
oldest daughter.

A moment of
forgiveness with my
youngest daughter.

Chapter 5

THE FLAWED MAN'S PLAN MARCHES ON

When we arrived at Ft. Riley in November 1982, we discovered once again that there was no Army housing available for us right away, despite it being one of the largest military installations in the United States. So, we had to move into a trailer park near Ft. Riley. A single wide, our mobile home was older, worn, and definitely lived in. The outside walls were metal, the inside walls were wood paneling, and there was just enough room for my mother to have her own bedroom while our daughter stayed with us in our bedroom. It wasn't what I had in mind, but it was sufficient.

We were told it could take up to six months to get post housing, but thankfully, we got ours in just two. We moved into a spacious, clean, and well cared for two-story condominium with wood flooring, two bathrooms, and three bedrooms that allowed momma and our daughter to have their own rooms. Even though I was receiving increased sergeant pay, finances remained tight, so Erica worked part-time at the Ft. Riley Post Exchange as a cashier and stocker. As we'd hoped, momma did a good job watching over our daughter, and she and I had some wonderful moments together going shopping or walking together at the park. Momma often shared how proud she was of me for being a good leader in the Army and for taking care of Erica, our daughter, and my son in Louisville.

But it was clear that momma's condition was deteriorating, and the stress of watching over her as the telltale signs of her mental illness slowly manifested themselves made it increasingly difficult to concentrate at work and give my family the attention they needed. She experienced short term memory loss and sometimes lost her temper for no reason. She occasionally had hallucinations about events that clearly did not occur.

We didn't feel our daughter was in any danger with her, but things couldn't continue as they were.

We finally arrived at the difficult emotional decision to send my mother back to Louisville to live with my second oldest sister in May 1983. Two other factors also contributed to the choice. First, we anticipated that I'd eventually get orders to leave the States for a second tour of duty in Germany. Second, we knew that momma needed to receive further psychiatric outpatient care that couldn't be provided at Ft. Riley because she wasn't my legal dependent. Junction City, the town outside of Ft. Riley, had a facility that offered occasional outpatient care and weekend activities for momma, but we could not find the higher level care and counseling she needed.

The day we put momma on a Greyhound bus back to Louisville was very sad. We had no other option for her travel. Erica and I couldn't afford at the time to drive or fly her back, and we determined that it would be safe enough to have her sit close to the driver to make sure she made the trip and was met by family upon arrival. Our daughter was just over a year-and-a-half old and had grown quite close to my mother in their time together.

She cried as my mother boarded the bus, and when we returned home, she walked into her grandmother's room looking for her. It was heart wrenching, but I assured our daughter that we would visit her again as soon as we could.

Erica and I were relieved. Momma was going to get the care she needed, and I felt I had done everything I could do in my situation to help her during those precious seven months. We also planned to see her whenever we took military leave to visit our families in Kentucky.

Momma loved me, and I loved her. Our time together had left no doubt about that.

Erica and I found a loving military wife to babysit our daughter when Erica was at work, and in June, I received another promotion and the increase in pay that came with it. That allowed Erica to later quit her job when our babysitter had to move overseas with her husband. We began to transition back into life with just the three of us, and it was nice. Although we missed my momma, we began to build some sweet memories. One of those was when we took our daughter to a nearby playground on a beautiful Midwest fall day. We packed a lunch, brought several toys, and relaxed in the sun as many other children played with our little girl.

As I neared my twenty-third birthday, I was a staff sergeant leading an entire squad in a battalion of about 500 soldiers. My rank, after a little over four years of service, was significant because that promotion came at a pace that fewer than one percent of enlisted personnel could achieve, setting me on a track for success. It was a huge achievement so early in my military career, and I was determined to make the best of it. I arrived early to work every day to set up our daily work schedule, and I made sure that I was the best dressed and most physically fit soldier in the entire battalion. Erica completely supported my efforts by ironing my fatigues nightly and ensuring my lunch was prepared in advance, all while taking care of the baby and keeping the house clean and organized. I shined my boots every night and laid out my fatigues and my index card notes with the next day's to-do list written on them.

Such diligence paid off. I was recognized several times for being the best soldier in the battalion by winning the in-ranks inspection, physical fitness competitions, and common skills testing. I started to make up for what I saw as my shortcomings handling my finances. I was able to begin saving money and paying off our debts. It was awesome! I was laser focused and starting to live out the promise I made to myself to be one of the best soldiers the Army had ever seen.

But that focus came at a cost. Erica had not yet fully grasped just how unusually driven I was. She believed in me and in my judgment and leadership, trusting that I always had goals and a plan for us as a family as well as for my military career. Yet over time, she began to recognize how my career goals and plans often overshadowed those for our family. She pointed out how I usually "had to do this" or "had to do that" as if there was no other choice when, in her mind, there were other options.

I told her that my motivation, in my heart and mind, was to progressively provide a better life for our family. In my defense, she understood that serving in the military, just as her father had for over 30 years, came with responsibilities that sometimes sacrificed personal and family time, energy, health, and if necessary, my life. Erica realized having a husband with a military career was not always conducive to raising a healthy family. She'd seen such realities in her own family with her mother.

Yet one of the main differences she saw between her father's military career and mine was that her dad did what was necessary to be a good soldier while still fully providing for his family's needs. When her father was home, he focused his time and attention on everyone, took care of things such as the yard and their vehicles, and helped her mother with responsibilities around the house.

On the other hand, when I was home, I set aside some time for Erica and our daughter, but I prioritized my military and educational goals. She occasionally opposed my decisions, suggesting that I was much more zealous in achieving the highest and best for my goals, but she didn't think they were always wise or necessary for the family. As time went on, Erica even began to feel that some of my military decisions were based more on selfishness, pride, and self-recognition rather than on simply having a successful career. She'd speak with me and insist that I reevaluate my decisions by seeking the underlying motivation for them and being more considerate to our family's needs and preferences.

I usually listened but generally didn't agree with her. Then I'd go ahead and follow through with my plans anyway. This became frustrating and irritating to Erica. She responded by continuing to pray for the Lord's will to be done instead of mine or hers. It became clear to her that God had designed me to be who I was, so she had to trust God and believe that He knew what He was doing and that He had a greater plan for me and for our family.

On top of all that, succeeding at work was proving to be a lot more difficult than I realized. I began using curse words whenever I got frustrated with the soldiers who didn't do what

I asked them to do. It seemed to work for other leaders in the Army. I also found myself becoming a true workaholic, routinely and willingly putting in longer hours than necessary in my drive to have the best missile systems repair team, all the way down to the best-looking barracks. I thought that was the only way to make it to the top in the Army and earn a reputation as a rock-hard soldier who accomplished any mission or task in an outstanding, exemplary fashion.

As a result, I started becoming harsh with Erica and our daughter. I criticized my wife when I came home and thought the house wasn't clean enough in comparison to the exacting standards I expected of my squad at work. I often spoke to her in a mean tone, especially when our daughter was ill, and she was sick quite often. As a baby, she had ear infections and lost weight every time she had one. After those infections cleared up, she developed severe asthma which caused her to get ill every month and lose more weight because she couldn't keep any food down. Her weakened immune system was further impacted by allergies and upper sinus issues. It was a constant cycle, and I did not show the patience I should have with our sick child.

Arguments increased between Erica and I, and a few times she got so frustrated she became mildly physical, poking a finger into my chest or something similarly non-violent. While I was not physically harmful in any way, I was mentally and emotionally hurtful, sometimes to the extreme.

I was too busy. I was too distracted. I was trying to be the best at everything!

But I was doing it all wrong—and it came to a head one unforgettable Saturday morning while Erica was still working. As usual, I had worked late that Friday night at our barracks ensuring that it was literally the cleanest on Ft. Riley. The Army uses the term "G.I. Party" to describe soldiers cleaning their living quarters, and everyone, squad members and their leaders, took to this task with gusto. In this instance, I was upset because our area of the barracks had just failed a cleanliness inspection. I wasn't going to have it.

Never mind it was Friday night. Never mind it was pay day. They were never going to embarrass me again as their leader. I was going to show them who was the boss!

When I finally got home at about 10:00 p.m., I was frustrated, on edge, and very sleepy. Erica woke me up early that next morning.

> I was trying to be the best at everything!

"What is it?" I grumbled.

"Don't you remember?" my wife gently reminded. "I have to go to work. You need to watch our daughter."

I sighed, undoubtedly a bit louder than I should've, and dragged myself out of bed to assess the situation.

Our daughter always woke up early. She loved cartoons.

My strategy became clear.

Erica left, and I took our daughter downstairs to the television. I fixed her a bottle of milk and then laid her down on a blanket on the floor in front of the TV. Pillow in hand, I plopped myself down next to her.

But I had forgotten a key tactic of my strategy. I hadn't checked to make sure the front door was closed and locked. Exhausted, I drifted off while my daughter was watching her Saturday morning cartoons.

She had started walking when she was nine months old and was quite mobile. She was also pretty stealthy, because the next thing I knew, I was waking up, and I didn't see her smiling face beside me.

She was gone.

Adrenaline surged, and I panicked! I ran from room to room. She was nowhere in sight. Those options exhausted, I looked at the front door and noticed it was slightly open. She had never opened the front door before, but she must have observed us turning the knob and figured it out.

Quickly, I bolted outside—and I saw her.

She was all the way at the end of our street next to a busy intersection.

A neighbor was with my daughter and appeared to be looking for her parents.

Guilt consumed me. When Erica returned home, all I could do was tell her how lousy a husband and father I was to have allowed our daughter to wander out of our home and into the streets. I apologized to her and to the neighbors. I also apologized to our daughter, and I have repeated that apology to her a number of times since that day.

It still scares me to think of what might have happened to her because of my gross negligence. Nothing like that ever happened again, and I am now known for my over-the-top care for anyone I am responsible for, especially children.

Another negative byproduct of my workaholism and fanatical drive to be the best soldier ever was my Christianity. I was straying from my newfound faith in Jesus, willing to pay the price to make it to the top in the Army at the expense of my family and God. Both were a distant second place in my life, and I was so ashamed. To coin an old Pentecostal term, I was placing Erica and my daughter on the altar just so I could pursue being a successful career soldier.

Still, I didn't realize how far I had fallen away as a new believer in Christ until the day I got drunk with some Army buddies. I had invited them over to the house for a casual dinner at the same time one of our neighbors was having a cookout. We were invited over, and I decided to join the two parties together without saying anything to Erica. She got upset, saying it was rude to invite my buddies over to our home, just to take them over to someone else's party. She had planned and prepared food for us, and I just pooped all over her hard work.

She told me in no uncertain terms that I was wrong, but I left with my friends anyway.

When I returned home later, I was quite inebriated. I was wobbly and my speech was slurred. Erica met me at the door, and even in my state, I could see the daggers in her eyes. I managed to get inside and start upstairs before we began arguing right there on the landing in the middle of the stairwell. Erica was so confused, disappointed, and angry with my rash decision making, she grabbed the front of my shirt, and pulled it toward her a little bit.

The motion wasn't much, but I was woozy, and when the shirt gave way in her grasp, I was knocked off balance.

I tumbled down the stairs.

It was only about six steps, and I was in good physical condition, so I wasn't hurt in any way by the fall. But her reaction certainly got my attention.

I got up and instantly began apologizing.

"I'm so sorry. I love you so much. This will never happen again."

It all spilled out in one sentence, I was so surprised and desperate to make amends. Erica didn't say anything, though. She just came down, turned, and went into another room. I had sense enough not to follow her. Instead, I staggered into the living room, plopped down onto the couch, and tried to get my thoughts together. After a while, I went into the bedroom, got down on my knees, and started praying. I begged God to forgive me and to allow me to find a way to be a good soldier and maintain my Christianity at the same time.

Eventually, I got into bed and fell asleep. Erica came in sometime later. We talked about what had happened the following morning.

It was a pivotal turning point in my life. It galvanized me as a person and made me realize that if I wanted to be a genuine Christian, I was going to have to strive to live a holy life, starting with owning my bad behavior.

I had to work on my weaknesses.

Those two events compelled me to formally recommit and rededicate my life to God. In October 1983, Erica and I were invited to attend a local Pentecostal church, the Church of God of Prophecy, by one of my co-workers. He was a good friend in my unit who had noticed how I was struggling with living out my faith. During the service, the young pastor spoke about how to live in the world and not be lost in it. He taught about how to grow as a Christian and overcome our mistakes in life.

As I sat in the church pew, his message hit my heart dead center, and I felt such deep sorrow that I knew I needed to repent. The pastor called people up to the altar in front of the platform to pray, and I went up. I asked Christ to forgive me, finally deciding that I had to stop tormenting myself for my many past sins of fornication, alcohol and marijuana use, laziness, and lying by hiding the full truth from others.

It was incredibly emotional. I had backslidden while I was trying to lead my family as a Christian man. I was so disappointed in myself that I knew I needed to rededicate my life to Jesus in order to become the person I wanted to be. I understood that Satan would not give me up without a fight, but I just had to remember where my strength came from and exercise my Christian faith with the same zeal I had demonstrated to become a good soldier in the Army.

Erica, who attended church services with me because it seemed to be a good and right thing to do, sat in the pew and observed it all. She didn't see herself as being a sinner and did not yet understand her need for salvation. But she saw that, whatever it was that was happening in my heart and mind, I was trying to be a better person, and that was fine with her.

We joined that church and denomination a few weeks later. I also began reading my Bible every day along with daily devotions from the book, Our Daily Bread. I started being conscious about my faith in God.

Sure, I knew then that there were still other spiritual battles to come, just as I know today there will be more battles yet to fight.

But I was just 23 years old, and I realized that I needed to recognize and admit to my shortcomings and learn how to grow from them.

I just didn't anticipate how difficult that was going to be.

Christmas found us back on track as a couple and filled with new hope for our relationship and our future. Erica had always been a kind and forgiving person, but both of those traits had been sorely tested since our arrival at Ft. Riley. She'd seen it all: the setbacks, the turnarounds, and everything in between. I'll always treasure that Christmas Eve, watching our daughter as she played near the tree with one of her brand new toys, a little plastic off-white pony with its long mane of blue and white hair.

She looked up, smiled at me, and Erica and I hugged. I almost cried for joy about having such a peaceful and loving home.

The following spring, I received orders to be reassigned back to Germany for a second two-year tour of duty, but not before being given a directive for temporary training lasting one month back at Redstone Arsenal in Alabama in May 1984. I was due to receive another level of missile systems repair knowledge to become an expert at repairing the Bradley Fighting Vehicle missile systems package. I was so excited to be one of the first soldiers educated on fixing the TOW anti-tank missile system. It convinced me that the Army was investing in me for potentially bigger and better opportunities to serve the country.

> I almost cried for joy about having such a peaceful and loving home.

During that month back at Redstone Arsenal, Erica and I continued to grow in our love for one another, and our daughter was less ill than she had been before. We attended a local Church of God of Prophecy on Sundays and Wednesdays, the only congregants of color in the entire church. However, we always felt welcome, and one of the older ladies at the church began to treat us as if we were her family.

When we returned to Germany in June, we again chose not to be command sponsored so that we wouldn't have to be away from the States and our families for three full years. This time, I was stationed at the Aschaffenburg Army Airfield. It was about 90 minutes east of Frankfurt where another one of Erica's six sisters lived with her husband, a sergeant major in the Army, and their two children. Twelve years older than Erica, she had lived with Erica for a while prior to getting married herself.

While Erica and our daughter stayed with her sister's family in Frankfurt, I settled in with my unit and found us a small but nice apartment off-base in Aschaffenburg. I stayed in temporary officer's housing until I secured the apartment. I also purchased a car a few days after we arrived, and I visited Erica and our daughter in Frankfurt on the weekends until we moved into the apartment. Even after we moved in, Erica spent as much time as she could with her sister in Frankfurt, thoroughly enjoying her family which included her nine-year-old daughter and seven-year-old son. Everyone there loved our daughter, who was pre-school aged for much of our time in Germany. They often invited us to their home for fellowship and her sister's good cooking.

Our little attic apartment was upstairs from a precious older German widow named Katherina, but we addressed her as "Oma," German for "grandmother." She was very kind and treated us like family. She didn't speak English and Erica was still just learning German, so they communicated the best they could and laughed whenever they misunderstood each other. Oma absolutely loved our little girl and always made sure she was well taken care of, giving her goodies and occasionally inviting us to eat with her. We ended up keeping in touch with her for many years via letters Oma's niece would interpret until Oma passed away. Oma was priceless. Our family, and friends like Oma, made our life in Germany very enjoyable.

I also found an international Church of God of Prophecy congregation in Langen, Germany. It was an hour-and-a-half drive each way, but it was more than worth the effort. I saw it as a God thing since not all American churches were available in Germany. We went most every weekend throughout our two-year stay, and the folks at the church were very loving to us. I began to grow more in my knowledge of the Word of God and further deepened my relationship with the Lord.

Not surprisingly, I was particularly interested in scriptures that spoke about how to obtain full repentance for past sins by admitting them to your loved ones, no matter how painful it may be to them. Central to that was 1 John 1:6-10. "If we claim to have fellowship with him and yet walk in the darkness, we lie and do not live out the truth. But if we walk in the light, as he is in the light, we have fellowship with one another, and the blood of Jesus, his Son, purifies us from all sin. If we claim to be without sin, we deceive ourselves and the truth is not in us. If we confess our sins, he is faithful and just and will forgive us our sins and purify us from all unrighteousness. If we claim we have not sinned, we make him out to be a liar and his word is not in us."

At the same time, I really enjoyed my new unit and working on the Bradley missile systems package. I was in charge of a vital mission for the Army's success in the European Theater, ensuring that all package systems for the Twenty-Sixth Support Battalion Third Infantry Division Europe were "all tests go" at all times in case of an attack from the then-Soviet Union or other Cold War combatant countries in the region. I was also becoming known as one of the best missile systems technicians in the Army, in large part due to tutelage from Chief Warrant Officer Two Gary Estes. His decision to hand his legacy of knowledge off to me was one of my greatest honors as a soldier.

Everything was going great—on the outside. Internally, though, I was in a new spiritual battle. As I learned more about what the Bible said and drew closer to God, the Lord started to challenge me to greater levels of accountability and vulnerability. When the pastor spoke one Sunday about being honest and confessing all of our sins not just to God but to anyone we may have hurt, even without their knowledge, his message penetrated my heart in a way I didn't expect.

I became convicted to fully admit and own up to my sins before the Lord—and to Erica. His text that Sunday, which just happened to be 1 John 1:6-10, inspired me anew. I wondered, *How was I going to lead my family and others while secretly keeping the full truth from my wife?*

I became convinced that it was time for me to mature and take on the full responsibility of being a Christian man. But I also knew I was going to find out if Erica really loved me enough to accept all of my past sins and some more recent ones. I fervently prayed to God, through His Son Jesus, to help me end the cycle of failed marriages in my family and break the chains of hiding my shortcomings from the love of my life.

The next evening, I came home from work. I walked in the door as Erica fixed dinner in our small kitchen while our daughter played in the living room. I was so nervous I almost talked myself out of making a full confession to her, telling myself that I was the only one that knew the full truth and no one would ever find out. But the Holy Spirit gave me the courage and strength to do what I had to do: fully repent of my sins to my wife.

Erica took one look at me and saw my trepidation. "What's wrong?" she asked.

I was trembling as I prepared to speak. "I need to tell you something," I announced.

We sat down at the kitchen table—and I revealed anything and everything that I had done, past and recent, that were sins before God and Erica. I shared all the details and corrected any half-truths I had told or tried to hide. I was in tears, and so was Erica. I tried to look her in the eyes, but I often had to glance away as the guilt of my confessions spilled out. I was afraid to see her reaction.

When all had been said, I closed with an apology. "I am truly sorry for not being completely honest with you this whole time."

The look on her face almost broke me. It was clear that Erica was very hurt. She told me several times along the way that she felt I had betrayed her and that she was angry at me. She later revealed that she, at one time, thought that I was almost perfect and could do no wrong. She had always looked up to me, and she was so happy and thankful to be with me.

Now, her eyes had been opened to reality. Erica couldn't understand how I could do such things, how I could be so deceptive, and how I could break her heart. She made it clear that she would never have done those things to me.

Over the next few weeks, Erica started having almost hateful feelings toward me and began treating me meanly. At some point every day, she had to fight the anger welling up within her. Such thoughts and feelings permeated her entire worldview about me, marriage, and even God. She ignored me and did not believe anything I said. She stopped smiling at me and gave me the cold shoulder. She found herself making snide remarks and acting like she didn't care about me or my feelings.

I had obeyed God, but I was devastated.

Erica no longer trusted me because I had betrayed that trust.

True leadership starts at home—and as leaders we must understand that there are consequences for our actions and behavior. Every relationship will go through crucibles like the one Erica and I were facing, but if we know our weaknesses and strengths as husbands and wives, marriages can survive these challenges. However, that is much more difficult to do without Jesus. Satan will always try to break up marriages. That is his job, so we have to be strong in our faith and put on the full armor of God to be able to battle him daily (Ephesians 6:10-18). We have to become consistent and persistent in our relationship and in raising our children. We don't have to be perfect. But we need to give all of our endeavors our best effort if we want to overcome such challenges in life and reach Heaven one day!

For Erica and me, our marital challenges came early in our relationship—and we both decided not to quit on each other. As I went through the pain, I was able to move forward because I had followed God's guidance, and I was a soldier. I knew that all I could do was take one step after the next and continue to stand as a growing Christian, even with my sinful past lingering in my life. My greatest challenge was seeing the hurt that I had caused the young woman that I loved with all of my heart, hoping that she would eventually be able to forgive me. Most people in this world, particularly non-Christians, would minimize my sins, but what God calls a sin is a sin—period.

Erica and I continued to love one another even when it was hard.

About two months after my revelations to Erica, we were at a special church service featuring the military chaplain who had also attended one of our church services in Langen. As he began sharing his message on prayer and forgiveness, preaching about repentance and turning our hearts toward Jesus, Erica remembers weeping as the chaplain asked if anyone was hurting or needed prayer. Anger, frustration, and brokenness churned away in Erica's heart, and at the close of the service, she went up to the altar in front of the main platform. She couldn't stop sobbing. I was sitting up front in my pew as I always did, wondering what she was going to do next.

Others gathered around Erica and began to pray for her. As some of them asked Erica if she wanted to confess her sins, she became frustrated. She hadn't done anything wrong. If anyone needed more prayer for repentance, it was me, not her.

Eventually, Erica was left alone at the altar, still crying. That's when the military chaplain reached down and began praying over her. At that moment, Erica realized that God was speaking to her heart and asking her to forgive me. As Erica put it later, "God revealed to me that I was a sinner, too. I wasn't perfect. I had hurt people. I had lied. I was no better than Harry. Even though I didn't cause him the same kind of pain he caused me, my thought life and my treatment of my parents and others was sinful just the same. I needed to own up to it and repent."

It was as though a huge light turned on in her heart and mind, and it all made sense. Erica felt the heavy, dark load of hate, anger, and frustration lift away. She began weeping over her own sins, repented, raised her hands and head, and started praising God for saving her soul. She said, "I previously didn't understand how wretched and sinful I actually was! I felt badly about hurting my parent's feelings and betraying their trust—but this was about my relationship with Jesus. I understood that I had sinned against and betrayed Him, and I was truly very, very sorry."

The same words from 1 John 1:6-10 that had encouraged and enlightened me began to take Erica through the process of true forgiveness, as did Christ's own words from Matthew 6:14-15. "For if you forgive other people when they sin against you, your heavenly Father will also forgive you. But if you do not forgive others their sins, your Father will not forgive your sins."

A darkness Erica had never really recognized or understood started to fade away in the blazing light of God's love and forgiveness.

As it did, Erica forgave me—and we began to heal.

That healing, and the growth in our faith that it nurtured, resulted in a calling from God to both of us to have a proper, official church wedding. I wanted to legitimize our marriage before the Lord and witnesses at the Church of God of Prophecy, but I also saw it as a fulfillment of part of my promise to make things right with Erica's family, as much as was possible, knowing that we had made decisions that hurt them. Erica's sister in Frankfurt was particularly excited because she had a friend who could make a wedding cake for us, and our church family was also thrilled to help and participate.

Our pastor officiated the basic ceremony on June 30, 1985, in front of the full church congregation and some of my military friends and family members. Approximately 50 people were there, and one of my Army sergeants was my best man while his wife served as Erica's maid of honor. Both were very good friends to us, and they had three beautiful little girls who loved to play with our daughter. Erica had just turned 22, and I was going to be 25 a few days later in July. We all had a wonderful celebration together as we were married God's way and with His blessing instead of in a courtroom. My greatest memory of our church wedding was Erica walking down the aisle in her beautiful wedding dress with a big smile on her face. She said she could feel God smiling down on us as we ventured together, both as husband and wife and as a son and daughter of God.

> Erica forgave me—and we began to heal.

Most military bases in Europe had an office that planned trips throughout Europe for military members and their families. Through that office, I had heard about a trip to Spain a few months earlier and had started saving funds for the trip as a surprise for Erica. She was also able to save a little money to help us pay for it by working at the local Post Exchange store as a cashier. Erica's sister watched our daughter at her home while we were on our five-year belated honeymoon. We traveled by bus, and we stayed in Spain for five days.

On the way we stopped in France for lunch, and I can still remember the flies that kept bothering us as we ate outside at a picnic table at a hotel rest stop. Under beautiful blue skies spotted by fluffy white clouds near a path of lush, green fruit trees, Erica and I enjoyed bread, different cheeses, and a selection of cold meats as a warm breeze brushed our faces. We reflected about how far we had come as individuals and as a couple, and we thanked God for allowing us to see parts of the world that we both used to dream about as children growing up in financially struggling homes. I also thought about how fortunate I was to have a career in the Army that allowed me to take care of my family while being able to visit such incredible places.

In Spain, we spent most of our time on the beautiful beaches of Costa Brava, and we also visited the Catalonia town of Lloret de Mar and the bustling city of Barcelona that would ultimately host the 1992 Summer Olympics. We saw gorgeous sites such as a medieval castle, Castell de Pals, where we watched jousting knights. We also attended bull fights in the Catalan countryside outside Costa Brava and went dancing at a cool disco in Lloret de Mar named Disco Tropics. As we entered the club and "Tarzan Boy" by Baltimora blared from the huge speakers hanging from the ceiling, I couldn't help but think back to when Erica and I first met at a far different type of disco in the States.

We had lots of fun together. One day, we paid for an excursion to take a ride in a glass bottomed boat, and we floated past some men standing on a small island in nothing but their birth-day suits. It was quite a day. We also accidentally stumbled upon a partially nude beach near our hotel when the beach we nor-mally went to was packed with summer tourists. It was a bit of a shock, and like the island, one we were swift to move on from. There was also the time when a man came up to us near our hotel, opened his jacket, and revealed a large selection of watches displayed neatly in the lining of his coat. He asked me if I wanted a nice watch. Assuming they were probably stolen, I politely declined, and we quickly walked away.

Our trek through an exotic country like Spain was a far cry from splitting a three-piece chicken meal from KFC, though, admittedly, the meal was a bit cheaper. Most significant, how-ever, was that Erica and I had begun enjoying each other's com-pany again and had continued to move beyond the anger of the past. We were so very thankful.

Upon our return, I continued growing into a more professional soldier. As I matured spiritually and emotionally, I better recog-nized my weaknesses and strengths and began to work on each one a little every day. I read Army technical manuals, ate a more balanced diet, and worked out more often. I eventually scored best in my battalion of almost 1,000 soldiers on my skills quali-fication test, and I fired expert at the rifle range and earned excel-lent marks on my physical fitness test. I also began to compete in and win several soldier competitions such as non-commissioned officer of the quarter, the common task test, the ruck march, and land navigation.

I was motivated to win these competitions not so much for my ego, but because I knew they led to promotions that would allow me to save money so I could take better care of my family and extended family—and become the first one in my family to attend and graduate from college. I wanted to break what I saw as the "generational curses" of my family such as poverty, divorce, and lack of education. The way I saw it, I had sinned and failed enough in my young life, and I wanted to change my path going forward! I was a little more consistent and persistent each day, thinking differently about who I was and who I was becoming. Finally, I wanted to ensure that I was representing Jesus in everything I was doing in the Army while being humble and appreciative for the opportunities God was allowing me to experience.

In the fall of 1984, I had been asked by my company commander to represent our battalion by competing in the prestigious Sergeant Morales Club selection process. Established in 1973 by Lt. Gen. George S. Blanchard to promote the highest ideas of integrity, professionalism, and leadership for the enlisted forces serving in Europe, gaining membership into the club is a rigorous and competitive event. It was well known that those selected received an early promotion to their next rank and some of the better assignments in the Army. Competitors had to go through several military boards at different levels and answer questions on all things Army and Army history, pass hands-on weapon tests where we had to pick up a weapon, disassemble it, and assemble it within a certain time limit, and pass land navigation tests and in-ranks inspections. The entire process lasted nearly a year—and in the end, I was chosen as one of the youngest non-commissioned officers ever to be selected in the history of the program!

In all, the second tour of duty in Germany was a complete success personally and militarily. Before it ended, I was also approached to consider becoming a warrant officer, and in early 1986, I received my orders to report to Ft. Stewart, Georgia in July. A few months before that, in November 1985, I was also notified that I was selected to receive a promotion to sergeant first class, another rare, almost unheard of, early promotion. In my MOS, no one had ever received that promotion level quicker than I did.

The ultimate goal, though, was college. If I ever wanted to truly excel in the Army, I needed to earn at least an associate's degree. With that in mind, I started my first college level course right after we had arrived in Germany, and I never looked back. I continued taking classes at night from then on—and I am blessed to say that in 1998 I became the first warrant officer in the history of the U.S. Army to obtain a doctorate level degree. I had proven to myself, by the grace of God and the support of a good Christian woman, that maybe my flawed plans to succeed in life could come to pass along with God's plans for me and my family.

As Erica and I headed back to the United States, my belief was clear: I was on track, and I would stay that way, as long as I continued to serve God and live for Him.

The lessons I was going to learn next were nothing short of excruciating and amazing.

Chapter 6

THE FLAWS GET MORE PERSONAL

We took leave before transitioning to our next post at Ft. Stewart, during which we visited our families. We started with Erica's family in Radcliff and Ft. Knox: her parents, three sisters and their husbands, and some nephews and nieces. Then we headed to Louisville to see my son at his mother's apartment. After that, we planned to see Big Mama and Big Daddy, along with my aunt and uncle, a couple of cousins, and some of my brothers and sisters who lived in the area. That included a trip to see my momma, who by then was once more institutionalized.

Our trip to see my son was a particularly important visit since he had not spent much time with his sister over the last few years. During that visit, his mother told Erica and I, in no uncertain terms, that we could no longer see my son. She has decided to solidify her hold on him by ending our influence in his life.

As we drove away after that visit, I wondered what was going to happen to my son. That night, I prayed that someone would intervene in his life and help him find faith in God one day, as so many others had done in my life.

In the days that followed, I became saddened whenever I thought about my son. At the very heart of who I am, I do not want to leave anything undone. I try to clean it up. I strive to accept my lot and make it better. I never wanted to perpetuate what I saw as an African American curse of children without fathers, but sadly, I had added to that curse.

It could have been much worse. I could have walked away from my son at the very beginning. I wasn't a saint, but I attempted to have a real relationship with him. But his mother had all the cards, and I could only respond to what she allowed.

Much later, I learned that it had been communicated to my son that *I* was the one who left because I didn't want to be his father and spend time with him. That was unfortunate. Although I had once questioned if I really was his biological father, I had made peace with those thoughts, and I operated as though I *was* his father. Why else would I have attempted to build a relationship between him and the rest of my family?

From the time he was eight until he was 10, we sent gifts and money. We made phone calls. But we had no lasting influence in his life during those critical early years.

I was no longer in my son's life to be a male role model for him, but at least I knew he had his maternal grandparents to look up to. It wasn't like my son was living in a bad situation. In some ways, it gave him better odds of success than I had at his age.

It's a shame that none of that prevented him from making some very poor choices later.

Erica and I wouldn't see him again until 1992. By then, he had already begun getting into the type of life that would ultimately end it.

We arrived at Ft. Stewart and instantly encountered another bleak housing situation. We had to rent a trailer again until more housing units opened up on post—and we did so at the Horsecreek Trailer Park in Ludowici, Georgia. The landlord was an older, petite, little fireball of a lady named Mrs. Edenfield. There was no doubt she was in charge and called all the shots. She was waiting at the housing office, recruiting and strongly insisting that we and other newcomers become her new tenants. All we were expected to say was, "Yes, ma'am!"

Ludowici was a long, winding 25-minute country drive away from Ft. Stewart past trees, dusty, unpaved roads, and a seemingly stagnant creek into what seemed like the middle of nowhere. However, Horsecreek was well-maintained and pristine. Mrs. Edenfield took us on a tour around the park, which featured a small, show horse track and arena before getting to the lot where the homes were situated in tidy rows. We were assigned the first trailer on the right, a metal, white and tan single-wide trailer with wood paneled walls. It was older but well kept, and the yard of dirt, rocks, and some grass with weeds was well groomed. Several similar homes with slight differences in color, size, and design made up the rest of the park. Mrs. Edenfield's consistent commentary about Horsecreek was, "Now, ain't that nass?"

Our home consisted of a main room at one end that was separated by a peninsula from the kitchen, which led into a narrow hallway down one end of the structure. Entrances to two small rooms, a bedroom and a bathroom, were along the hallway, which ended before a final larger room, our bedroom, at the far end of the house. The beautiful countryside around it was punctuated by the presence of Mrs. Edenfield's beautiful and obviously well cared for horses, most likely Quarter horses or

Morgan horses, one of which was a lovely, dark brownish/red that she rode.

We soon discovered that Mrs. Edenfield and her crew rode on horseback throughout the trailer park on a regular basis and peered through the windows of her tenants' homes in a very nosy fashion, invading our privacy with no qualms about it. It was very irritating, but we just had to live with it. When we saw her coming, we quickly pulled our curtains shut, but she was usually stealthy enough to sneak up on us unawares. Aside from that, we really liked Mrs. Edenfield. Erica couldn't help but feel that there was a sweet, precious soul underneath all of the leather and chaps she wore.

Before long, we realized that Mrs. Edenfield cared about us and the others under her residential care. There was a young, unwed single mother living in one of the trailers near Mrs. Edenfield's lovely stone and brick home. She was very concerned about this young lady who looked as though she couldn't have been more than 14, and even more worried about her toddler. She asked Erica—actually, it was more like she "voluntold" her—to visit the girl, check on her and the child, make sure they were okay, and then report back to her. Erica agreed, and discovered that the young lady was partially unresponsive, almost as if she had mental or emotional challenges, and was unable to properly care for her child.

We're not sure how Mrs. Edenfield specifically intervened, but a few days later, the girl and her child were no longer living there. Mrs. Edenfield not only wanted her property well taken care of, but she also wanted her tenants to be safe and cared for, and she did everything she could to prevent anything illegal, dangerous, or harmful from happening.

There was one other person from our arrival at Ft. Stewart that we'll never forget. His name was Brother Bill, a tall, precious, dear older brother who played the guitar and assisted in ministry at our tiny Church of God of Prophecy in Hinesville, Georgia, a sleepy little town right outside Ft. Stewart. We grew to love Brother Bill because he was so very friendly, loving, and caring.

One day during a series of revival services, one of the teenage girls from the small church brought a young man with her. He caught our attention because he was a handsome black gentleman. He was the first person of color we had seen in our church since we'd been there, and on top of that, he was the boyfriend of a white girl.

As the service continued, Brother Bill was in the middle of singing a song when he suddenly stopped and began sobbing. We had no clue what he was so upset about. The next thing we knew, Brother Bill got up, walked over to the young black man, and wrapped his old, white arms around him. "I'm sorry," he said over and over as he wept in the man's arms. "I'm sorry."

Brother Bill later explained that he had been raised to hate black people. He did not trust them, and he had mistreated them. He then said the Lord opened his eyes and his heart, revealing to him that he was wrong and that his upbringing was harmful. So, even though he didn't know the young black gentleman, Brother Bill felt that he had to repent to him and to God.

After that, we all sang together, rejoicing—and the lesson from that day remains in our hearts, proving the truth of Hebrews 4:12-13. "For the word of God is alive and active. Sharper than any double-edged sword, it penetrates even to dividing soul and spirit, joints and marrow; it judges the thoughts and attitudes of the heart. Nothing in all creation is hidden from God's sight.

Everything is uncovered and laid bare before the eyes of him to whom we must give account."

There is little that is easy about family life in the military, but Erica dealt with all of it with grace and wisdom. She learned how from her mother, who became a military spouse and left the Philippines and her dear, precious parents and family to make her own family with Erica's father in the States. Erica's maternal grandparents passed away before her mother was able to return home to visit them. While that was sad and difficult, Erica's mother tirelessly set an example of how it was appropriate, expected, and beneficial for the family to work together as a loving and caring team, sacrificing personal desires in the process. Her mother worked outside the home when needed, and whenever Erica's father was deployed, her mother had full responsibility to care for the family and every aspect of the household. Responsibilities were delegated to Erica and her siblings, with the older children keeping watch over the younger ones. Erica and her family went to church regularly, and while it was sometimes a bit boring to her, Erica got used to it and went without question.

Her mother taught us about having faith in God in all circumstances, as well as to be thankful in times of plenty and to trust Him in times of want. As an adult, and especially as a parent, Erica says she finally began to understand why her mother said and did what she did, and she greatly loved and highly respected and appreciated her parents for their faithfulness and love toward her, us, God, and others. They reminded Erica of the words of 1 Timothy 5:4 ("But if a widow has children or grandchildren, these should learn first of all to put their religion into practice by caring for their own family and so repaying their parents and grandparents, for this is pleasing to God.") and of 2 Timothy 1:5 ("I am reminded of your sincere faith, which first lived in your grandmother Lois and in your mother Eunice and, I am persuaded, now lives in you also.").

I was very fortunate to have a wife that understood how the military worked and one who supported me at a level very few military wives would for their spouses. My friends in the military often told me that Erica's support was one of the most valuable assets I could possibly have to be successful in the Army. Erica always asked me how my day went and to tell her what I had learned while working, eager to help me make myself into a better soldier and person. The fact that she still gets up to see me off to work, just as she has since we were married, makes her a hero to me!

Erica was a consistent support as I got underway with my duties at Ft. Stewart in June 1986 with excitement and gusto. My commander and warrant officers were impressed enough with my work to write and submit a letter of recommendation for me to become a warrant officer, an expert who specializes in one of the Army's 48 technical areas such as intelligence, aviation, engineering, and missile systems.

> I was very fortunate to have a wife who supported me at a level very few military wives would.

The process is not unlike enlisting or applying for officer candidate school. It starts with the Armed Services Vocational Aptitude Battery (ASVAB). It has 10 different scores, but the one that matters most is the general technical score that tests an applicant's aptitude to learn a technical trade. Once the ASVAB has been passed, the standard military physical examination comes next. If applicants wish to be aviators, they have to pass the flight physical performed by a military flight surgeon. Anyone wanting to be a warrant officer also has to pass the Army's specific physical fitness test to assess their strength and cardiovascular endurance. Once all of the required tests have been taken and passed, a formal application is filled out that may require the applicant to write a one-page paper on why they want to be a warrant officer.

More steps follow, including a potential interview before a formal board, and it can be a grueling process. Generally, established soldiers can only apply for warrant officer positions related to their current occupations, but there are exceptions where a different field can be applied for. I had to give up my enlisted rank and take a slight pay reduction to become a warrant officer candidate, but the bigger picture meant more compensation in the long run.

I sent in my completed packet. Right after that, in April 1987, I was pinned in an official ceremony as sergeant first class (the seventh of nine non-commissioned officer enlisted levels, and the first of three senior levels of rank) and began the eight-week Advanced Non-commissioned Officers Course (ANCOC) held at Redstone Arsenal. One of the youngest soldiers of that rank to attend ANCOC in ordnance corps history, becoming sergeant first class remains the most humbling promotion of my Army career because of how often I had placed my career ahead of my family to achieve that level of advancement.

At ANCOC, I was required to live in a two-soldier housing unit with a fellow senior non-commissioned officer during the course. Erica and our daughter left to stay with her mother so that I could more easily visit them each weekend in Radcliff, near Ft. Knox, rather than having to travel all the way to Ft. Stewart in Georgia. Each week, there was a barracks inspection that had to be passed in order to earn a weekend pass—and my roommate was a problem. He wasn't tidy, and he got drunk most every night. He barely cleaned his side of our living area, so I took it upon myself to help him so that we'd pass inspection and I'd be able to leave to visit Erica and our daughter.

Despite my best efforts, about halfway through the course, our room failed its inspection thanks to my messy roommate. During the doomed inspection, I told the inspector that I didn't think it was fair for my roommate's lack of discipline to affect my access to a weekend pass.

What I didn't know was that the inspector was not only friends with my roommate, but he was also his drinking buddy.

"You're not a team player," the inspector accused. "You should just clean any areas that need it if you want to keep going home."

So, for the remaining four weeks, I got up early and cleaned both sides of our living area before each inspection. As I did, I brooded over the unfairness of it all. I felt the inspector was an awful leader and unjust in his decision making. I believed my roommate was what we in the Army called a "dirtbag." But the whole ordeal informed me of an inconvenient truth. Some leaders in the Army were bad, and the experience reminded me of the poor leadership displayed by my lieutenant years earlier that had led to my face being burned. I just had to learn how to deal with them until I could rise to a rank high enough to replace them. I never forgot that experience, and I have tried to remember the lessons of how unjust it is to administer mass punishment and how improper relationships between senior leaders and their subordinates can negatively affect others.

In the end, I passed the ANCOC course and reaped the benefits of being a sergeant first class. Soldiers with that rank and above received more respect and more institutional Army power. They also got better housing—and I was not just offered Army housing, but available options that were usually only offered to sergeant majors. That allowed Erica and I to move our family from the stately environs of the Horsecreek Trailer Park to a wonderful, almost brand-new, two-story condominium at Ft. Stewart. It had all new appliances, wooden floors, and a sliding glass door leading to a nice patio area. The neighborhood was well kept, and every lawn looked immaculate. We felt as if we were the hillbilly Clampetts moving from Bug Tussle to Beverly Hills.

Finally, being a sergeant first class allowed my family to receive improved medical treatment, and there were times officials at the base's health facility would allow me and my wife to go to the head of the line whenever we brought in our daughter for her monthly bouts with ear infections, fevers, or digestion issues. As we continued praying that one day she would move past her health issues, at least Erica and I could now get better care for her.

My performance at ANCOC had many of my leaders beginning to think that I could someday rise to sergeant major if I stayed focused and continued the track I was on. That made me feel validated for putting in the effort and sacrifices I had to succeed—and, as if in confirmation of their beliefs, I was selected to become a warrant officer as a technical expert in Land Combat Missile Systems in July 1987.

The first part of warrant officer training was at the Aberdeen Proving Grounds in Maryland. It was my opportunity to change the narrative of my professional life as an officer in the Army, and it felt like I was in a movie and becoming the star. I had been waiting my entire life to excel, and God was allowing me the chance to become a leader of men and women for the defense of the United States. I strived to keep it all in perspective, remembering the exhortation from 1 Peter 5:6. "Humble yourselves, therefore, under God's mighty hand, that he may lift you up in due time."

When I arrived at Aberdeen in November 1987, my head was still spinning from making sergeant first class so early and graduating ANCOC. As I was processed, the warrant officers in charge read my military file and noticed that I had held several leadership positions during my enlisted career in addition to my previous promotions. I overheard one of the Training, Advising, and Counseling (TAC) officers tell his coworker that I should be closely observed to possibly be chosen as the class leader.

A few days later, our class of new warrant officer candidates officially began training, and the class' TAC officers chose someone else to be the class leader. I was a little saddened, but I quickly got over it, determined to help the chosen class leader succeed. I understood that I couldn't be a great leader unless I was a great follower, too. During the first few weeks, our class was given little to no time in the evenings to clean the barracks and prepare our uniforms for school the next day. It was all part of the school's time management and teamwork training to see if classes could come together and collaborate to take care of the barracks and get uniforms ironed and boots shined while still completing nightly homework assignments.

I suggested that our class set up teams of people with specific jobs to accomplish these tasks each night. It worked out great, and everyone, including the class leader, loved my idea and wholeheartedly supported it. We even had enough time left for me to conduct a nightly Bible study before mandatory lights out at 10:00 p.m.

About halfway through the training at Aberdeen, I was catapulted to class leader after a series of shortcomings were revealed that worked against the class leader and his leadership team. Once I became class leader, we chose a class motto. After fielding suggestions from my fellow classmates, my recommendation of "To the Top, Sir" was chosen and embroidered on our class guidon flag. I led our class to graduate on time and receive high grades on our final inspection. Due to its small size, news traveled fast in the warrant officer corps that I was a go-getter and could get things done.

I completed phase one warrant officer training at Aberdeen and started phase two, the technical component, back at Redstone Arsenal. That took eight months and consisted of hands-on training on all of the missile systems in the land combat Army inventory. I studied long hours every night on each technical aspect of the missile systems and their testing equipment. I was also graded on physical fitness and in-ranks inspections. I always told myself, "No one can out fitness me, out shoeshine me, or out work me!" I did my best to own my level of effort and engagement. Although I was super competitive in any and all things having to do with the Army, I never did so at the expense of making a fellow soldier look bad.

I was in my wheelhouse being a full-time missile systems student and challenging myself to better develop my leadership traits. I started to believe my own outlandish dreams that I would become one of the best warrant officers in the history of the U.S. Army. Meanwhile, I ran into the same inspector from ANCOC who had shown such poor leadership. He observed me in the Ordnance School Academy hallway one day and tried to avoid me when he noticed it was me, realizing that I had advanced to the second phase of my warrant officer training.

I caught up to him, and I told him that I would never forget his poor leadership and would strive to be a better leader than he was. I then wished him well and walked away.

All through my training, Erica carried on with our daughter, taking incredible care of her so all I had to do was go to school and study while I was home during the week. On Saturdays, we took our daughter to the park or to the theater to see a Disney movie, then we went to church together as a family on Sunday.

At the end of the course, I was selected as the honor graduate and pinned as Warrant Officer One Harry Hobbs. I will never forget that feeling. It validated me and my strategies on how to achieve success in the Army.

I believed I was on my way for sure!

During this time in my life, my movie was playing itself out nicely. It's easy to assume that my thinking and behavior was over the top as I pursued accomplishments in an extreme manner. But I grew up in poverty with very little, so my mindset was simple. I believed that I had to give every ounce of my effort toward my Army career because there was no Plan B for me to be able to succeed in life and provide for my family.

I believed I was on my way for sure!

My next tour was at Ft. Hood near Killeen, Texas. Whenever we had to travel as a family to a new duty station, Erica and I packed up our Toyota Cargo Van to the hilt, and our daughter played quietly in her car seat with her little ponies. We arrived in August 1988, and true to form, Army housing was full. But God had the situation in His hands. Erica's older sister had retired in Killeen with her husband and kids, and they allowed us to stay with them for several weeks until we purchased a home nearby. We had been informed by the Army that we should be stationed at Ft. Hood for at least three years, so we felt it was time to buy a home for the first time and try to build up some equity as property owners. We quickly found a local Church of God of Prophecy and plugged into the congregation. In everything, Erica and I were trying to remain persistent and consistent in achieving and fulfilling our professional and spiritual goals.

We were inspired by two passages of Scripture. The first, 1 Corinthians 15:58, said, "Therefore, my dear brothers and sisters, stand firm. Let nothing move you. Always give yourselves fully to the work of the Lord, because you know that your labor in the Lord is not in vain." The second, 2 Timothy 2:15, exhorted, "Do your best to present yourself to God as one approved, a worker who does not need to be ashamed and who correctly handles the word of truth."

As you apply these truths to your life as a believer in God, you will solidify your integrity while pursuing all your goals in life. I have had daily, weekly, monthly, and yearly goals since the day I met Erica. As my motivation, she sharpened my senses and inspired me to become the best version of myself physically, spiritually, mentally, and financially. That added to my existing self-motivation that, even though I was only half black, I felt that I represented all people of color, especially African Americans, by making Army history as the first person of color in several key military positions. I had grown up reading books on the Civil War, slavery, and the civil rights movement, so I knew that God was blessing my career and allowing me to do better than I ever thought humanly possible as a biracial person in the military.

Today, I feel the same way serving in the corporate world in Alabama as the first person of color in several highly visible positions in Huntsville, a city crowned in 2022 by U.S. News and World Report as the best place to live in America.

At Ft. Hood, I was ready to launch my legacy as a warrant officer. However, I still had many flaws I was trying to work through. One of them was maintaining my integrity at all times regardless of the situation—and I was about to be reminded once more about the importance of unwavering honesty in my life.

One of the first duties I had when I arrived at my new unit was to qualify with my weapon at the M16 rifle range. I had never been good at shooting. Throughout my military career, I had always just barely hit the minimum number of targets to earn a passing score. But I was now an officer, and I badly wanted to impress my new command.

So, I decided to help myself along a bit by adding extra target hits onto my score sheet by punching holes in it with my military ink pen so that it would appear the holes were made by bullets fired from my rifle. It was cheating, pure and simple, but I chose to compromise my integrity in an effort to impress others instead of accepting the fact that I was a minimal performer at the range. I also allowed my prideful desire to be the very best to override the better choice to be honest in my decision making.

When I returned from the range that morning and the targets were collected, it was obvious I had cheated. The ink pen holes were slightly but noticeably larger than M16 bullet holes. The range officer took my altered target to my new company commander. At that time, she was one of the few females in the Army who had beat the odds to be in charge. She was very professional, and she was an extremely knowledgeable ordnance officer.

I was summoned into her office that very afternoon. I walked in and saluted.

She immediately read me my Miranda rights.

At that moment, I realized what it really meant to be an officer in the United States Army and the weight that responsibility carried. "Did you alter the target at the range?" she asked.

My response was vague and inexcusable. "I just did what I saw others doing at the range to increase their scores."

Not only was I denying my own responsibility, I was transferring the blame to others and lying in the process anyway.

"Mr. Hobbs," she repeated, "did you cheat at the rifle range today to increase your score?"

"Yes, ma'am," I replied, then came clean with my motives. "I did it because I wanted to impress you and others in the company today by scoring the best at the range."

"I am placing you on probation for possible Uniform Code of Military Justice punishment. I'll need to investigate further before I can administer disciplinary actions."

I was dismissed.

I went home and informed Erica of the horrible mistake I had made in my first assignment as a brand new officer. She had warned me not to cheat at the range like others she had heard me talk about, yet her look of disappointment came with words I desperately needed to hear. "I will support you through this ordeal." Erica also said she would pray for me to always be truthful when I was under pressure to not fail.

I was ashamed as a Christian and as an officer. After all I had been through in the Army and everything we had dealt with as a couple, I couldn't believe that I still struggled with my integrity. We prayed together, and I asked God to again forgive me of my many sins and my inability to overcome being dishonest.

Over the next six months, my commander gave me every tough additional duty in the company, including placing me in charge of all of the ranges our company operated. This allowed me to face my failure head on, learn how to be a competent range officer, and qualify with all handheld weapons. I was also put in charge of all arms room weapons and overall security for the entire company.

I was called into my commander's office, and she complimented me for performing all of the additional duties with integrity. We had installation level inspections on all of those areas and earned excellent scores. My commander also informed me that I was off probation and had regained her confidence.

"Never forget your lapse in judgment," she added, "and how hard it was for you to become an officer. Don't do anything else that could hurt your career because I feel you have the potential to become one of the best warrant officers I have ever known."

Redemption is incredible—and even more so when it has been genuinely earned.

Lesson learned, I continued to take on as many tough jobs as I could as a young officer. I wanted to get my hands dirty with the enlisted soldiers as they went about their daily tasks so I could learn from the bottom up how to do business as an officer. Normally, young officers, such as myself, were given leadership over these duties done by the lower enlisted, and I eagerly volunteered to provide oversight of as many of those jobs as possible. I was beginning to move toward my dream of becoming a senior officer, and ultimately, a commander with one goal in mind: to become one of the best officers in the history of the U.S. Army!

It wasn't egotistical. I just wanted to push myself to excellence so that when I retired I wouldn't be one of those veterans who talked about what they could have accomplished or should have done. I truly believed that I was standing on the shoulders of other people of color who had come before me in the Army but who didn't have the opportunities I was receiving. Erica's father was in the Army for 30 years but was never given the training or the opportunity to apply to become an officer. He always thought it was because he was black. Likewise, my brother, even though he joined the Army just one year before me, did not receive assignments that could have put him on a more successful track and enhanced his career. He also solely believed that was because he was black.

The Army certainly had to work through institutional racism—and I understood that I was a token. Did my mixed ethnicity give me promotions and opportunities that others didn't get? Possibly—but whatever the motivation, I decided that, with God's help, I was not going to waste a single one of them. I told myself that even if I was someone's token, I would be the best token they ever selected. I may not have been their first choice, but I wanted to show that I was the best choice.

I often recalled Romans 12:2, which declared, "Do not conform to the pattern of this world, but be transformed by the renewing of your mind. Then you will be able to test and approve what God's will is—his good, pleasing and perfect will." I had always attempted to be a student of African American history. I was particularly intrigued with learning as much as I could about the U.S. Civil War. It came in part from conversations I had as a youngster with Big Mama and Big Daddy. He had been called up for World War II, but he didn't deploy because the war ended prior to his unit being needed in Europe. As a result, I saw my military service, and my latest role as an officer, as being completely intertwined with God's desire for my life.

When I embarked on a genealogical search, 15 years later, near the end of my Army career, I discovered that my great, great maternal grandfather was born a slave in America after his father had been captured and brought over on a slave ship from Africa. A certified researcher found a copy of the manifest dated August 3, 1850—the same month, 138 years later, that I became an Army officer. I view coincidences like that as evidence of God's grand design for my life, even though I was flawed and still on my journey toward becoming the person God wanted me to be.

During that same search, I also discovered that another one of my distant African American relatives who was born a slave had been freed so he could fight for the Union Army in the Thirty-Fifth Regiment, Kentucky Infantry. His unit served honorably and helped the Union win the war over the Confederacy. Such vignettes from my personal history allowed me to look back and appreciate even more my service and education in the Army as a person of color—and it also inspired my current work in corporate America and in the community organizations I serve.

Our daughter was seven years old by the start of 1989, and her unique personality was starting to develop. Erica and I could tell she was going to be very smart but easily distracted and therefore needed a lot of attention—attention that I just didn't seem to have enough of to share with her. She was lonely and kept asking us to have a brother or sister for her to play with and to love.

Selfishly, I didn't want another child because I was struggling with being a father to one in my home and to my son who lived in another. However, she and Erica finally convinced me to agree to expand our family.

I thank God that they did—especially in light of what was going to happen next.

Chapter 7

THE FLAWED MAN GOES TO WAR

Our second daughter arrived in October 1989. She was born an officer's daughter into the officer's child's tradition. In accordance with one of the oldest Army rites, she got a silver cup with her name on it from my unit. We celebrated her arrival with Erica's sister and family who lived nearby. As we did, I hoped I would be an improved father this time around.

Our first year with her was awesome. I am a huge Batman fan, so when she was just an infant, I rented the movie *Batman* starring Michael Keaton and Jack Nicholson. One of my enduring memories is of her and I laying together on the floor watching that movie, and it planted a seed in her, too. As she grew older, she became a big Batman fan, and she even got a Batman tattoo on her arm when she became an adult.

Our older daughter loved to help her momma take care of her new little sister, rocking her to sleep at night, kissing her on her forehead, and telling her how much she loved her and had prayed for her to arrive healthy and strong. That made sense considering how much our first daughter had dealt with illness. Erica and I took our girls to the mall on Saturdays to watch them play in the kid's zone area before grabbing lunch with them at Chuck E. Cheese. It was wonderful for us to have enough time and money to be able to create such fun times together for our family.

As the time for my next scheduled military reassignment to Aschaffenburg, Germany approached, I had settled in as an officer, and we were stable and happy as a family, loving God and one another. The only blemish came whenever I thought about my son. I missed him, and I hoped he was well.

After arriving in Germany, I did my best to acquire military housing for my family, who were still in the States trying to rent or sell our home in Texas, and keeping up with my demands as a Land Combat Missile Systems Warrant Officer. My duty was to ensure that the TOW weapon systems on all Bradley fighting vehicles in the third brigade were successful, pretested, and ready for combat.

This was essential—because something big was brewing in the Middle East. On November 1, our unit was informed that we were going to deploy at some point in the future from Germany to the Middle East. That same day, President George H.W. Bush had likened Iraqi President and Dictator, Saddam Hussein, to Adolf Hitler. Days later, Iraqi officials vaguely declared that they were preparing for a "dangerous war" even as U.S. Secretary of State James Baker visited American troops in Saudi Arabia. Within a week of that, 100,000 U.S. troops were sent to the Persian Gulf. Events escalated, it seemed, on a daily basis.

With all of the uncertainty and knowing a deployment to the Middle East was coming, I decided to use my credit card to pay for a flight and a two-week-long visit for Erica and the girls. I was staying in temporary officer quarters at Aschaffenburg at the Graves Kaserne barracks, so the plan was for us to stay together in a small two-room quarters in a building on base that had a kitchenette, a tiny bathroom, and a bedroom equipped with a fold-out couch. It was like a studio apartment, and it would be cramped, but it would do considering the circumstances.

Yet by the time they arrived at Ramstein Air Base after a 12-hour flight, everything had fallen through. The two-room quarters was no longer available because of all of the additional military personnel being brought into the city, so there we were, loaded down with luggage and walking around the streets in Germany at nine o'clock at night with nowhere to go. We tried to find a hotel, but every one of them was full. That left us, quite literally, with no room at the inn and not even a stable available for lodging.

Thankfully, I was mentoring a young lieutenant, and God spoke to me to go to him and request to spend the night with him and his wife. They already had a government leased housing unit in the city outside Graves Kaserne. When I knocked on his door, he asked what was going on, and I told him. His wife wasn't home, and he thought about it for a few seconds before assuring us that she would be fine with us staying there. "You all come here. I'll make a place for you on the floor."

We gratefully accepted, and we remained with them for three more nights before a hotel room finally became available. It was another one of those many humbling events with housing issues that had occurred throughout my military career, this one coming at the worst possible time. Yet we found a solution and made the best of it.

I only got to see my family for a couple of hours each day. I was able to rent a friend's car for transportation, so I'd leave early in the morning, come home for lunch, and return late at night. But when we were together, it was precious. We'd get a late dinner in the hotel lobby restaurant. If I got home early, while the sun was still up, we'd walk to the local park and the kids would play with some cheap German toys we bought for them. It would take five years to pay off the debt from their visit, but some things in life are more important than money, and I didn't know if I would ever get to see them again.

Erica and the girls flew back to the States right before Thanksgiving. By the time President Bush offered to send Secretary of State Baker to Baghdad to meet with Hussein on November 30, I was leading my platoon of 63 soldiers, the largest in my company. We were busy earning qualifying scores with our M16 rifles at the shooting range and packing our vehicles, equipment, and tentage. We carefully inventoried everything to ensure we had all of our basic issue items. Each vehicle had to be loaded with a shovel, first aid kit, fire extinguisher and other safety equipment, camouflage netting, and any required components for that vehicle. Every soldier had to have camping gear, individual clothing and survival gear, and their personal items. Everyone had to have a trenching tool, canteen, pistol belt, helmet, gas mask, MREs (Meals Ready-to-Eat), and their weapon and ammunition. We had to be ready to be self-contained and self-sustaining.

Then, on December 1, the specific deployment assignment came—to Saudi Arabia in support of the First Marine Expeditionary Force. They did not state the exact day we had to load onto the C141 Starlifter Military Air Transport Service flight, but we were informed a few days later that we would be flying to an imminent war zone on Christmas Eve. My unit was one of the last ones chosen to go, and we would be in close combat support.

That would likely place us right at the front of the action.

I called Erica the first week in December to let her know about Saudi Arabia and the Christmas Eve deployment date. I was upbeat, and my mind was clear. "Hey, sweetheart! Whatever is gonna happen is gonna happen. God's got it. It's going to be okay. I love you!" Erica, however, was anything but upbeat and clear. For her, the call simply confirmed the bad news she knew was inevitable but that she hoped wouldn't happen. We called on the Lord, prayed for strength and encouragement, and did our best to leave it, and us, in His hands.

As I loaded onto the C141 in Nuremberg on December 24, it felt unreal, like I was in an action movie not knowing how the plot would turn out. We arrived in Saudi Arabia on Christmas Day 1990. When I walked off the aircraft, I gathered my platoon leadership into a circle. I prayed with them and for us, and I thanked God for His Son, Jesus, coming to earth in human form to die for our sins and give us the opportunity to believe in Him, so we could be forgiven and make heaven our home one day. I desperately missed my family, but I thanked God that I was alive that day.

I also became a TV star in that moment—or at least that's what my family in the United States said later on. CNN was there covering our arrival in Riyadh, and out of the thousands of soldiers there, I was the one called over to be interviewed on international television. I did remarkably well when you consider that I had no time to prepare my thoughts. On behalf of my fellow troops, I said that we hoped to save lives and to stabilize the region so it could be safe again. "We are here," I declared, "to root out a tyrant that is invading a sovereign country that is one of our allies." I added that we didn't have a choice. We didn't like going to war, but we had to protect our allies and our interests. "It is important to our world," I concluded.

Several other people and friends at home saw me as the interview was replayed all day long. For Erica, it was better than a phone call because seeing me on the screen somehow made me that much more real to her. Her eyes told her that, right then, I was alive and well, and that comforted her.

But I have to admit: people thinking I was a TV star was the biggest kick.

That day across the Atlantic at our home in Killeen, the surreal sense that Erica felt was similar to what I was experiencing in the Arabian desert. It wasn't the first time we had been apart on Christmas Day, but it was unlike any other. Erica and the girls tried to make the most of it by focusing on the true meaning of Christmas: celebrating God's great love in sending His Son, Jesus Christ, into the world. They read books and watched videos about Jesus and Christmas.

They had a little Christmas tree which Erica let the girls decorate with their own handmade ornaments, one of which included a picture of me. They fashioned cinnamon ornaments made out of glue, flour, and spices and shaped with cookie cutters, and then hung them on the tree. They weren't edible, but Erica said they smelled so good. My family also crafted four golden yellow stockings made from felt, cut into different Army boot shapes and sizes then glued together to form pouches. They decorated them with shiny ribbons, buttons, pictures, and bows. The largest was mine, with Erica's the next biggest, our oldest daughter's a bit smaller, and our toddler's the smallest. They were all hung on the wall in the living room because we didn't have a fireplace.

Their celebration was quite solemn and sad without me being there—Erica always says I bring all the fun! However, the girls were blessed with a few toys and clothes from Erica, for which they were thankful.

My wife was in unfamiliar territory, inundated with mixed emotions, mostly missing me and very concerned about my health and safety as well as that of my unit, the U.S. military, the country, and the world as a whole. She didn't have Google or any other means to research information in real time like we take for granted today, so she and her church family prayed a lot that week leading up to the new year. From Christmas through New Year's Day, we were in lockdown, and I was very busy. I was not allowed to communicate with Erica and the girls. She expected that to happen considering that we had just arrived for our deployment, but just the fact that it was between Christmas and New Year's Day added to Erica's frustration and sadness.

As 1991 dawned, Erica's concern grew. She had hoped against hope that I wouldn't be deployed to the Middle East, and she didn't like it one little bit that I was there. She was very nervous and scared because it was the first time I was in an actual war zone. She knew her parents had survived war. They had told her stories about it growing up, including one of her mother having to run through the jungle as a teenager to survive the Japanese attack on the Philippines in World War II. Her father didn't like to talk much about his experiences, but Erica learned enough to know that he had been in grave danger and that I was, too.

> As 1991 dawned, Erica's concern grew.

She tried her best to rest in her mother's reassurance that just as she and her father were still here, I would make it through as well.

The majority of young military spouses temporarily moved back home to be with their families during this difficult time, but some chose not to or were unable to do so. Erica was blessed to have one of her sisters in Killeen, and in addition to visiting with them, Erica joined with the remaining Army wives at Ft. Hood to support one another and pray. None of them had any idea what to really expect, and Erica's anxiety was magnified by the fact that she had a one-year-old and a nine-year-old to comfort and take care of. In addition, after I deployed, our oldest daughter, who had constantly battled with her health, began behaving differently. She had never been apart from me for that long. When she was younger, she was happy, playful, imaginative, and usually overflowing with zinging energy. One of her teachers rightly described her as a little social butterfly, bubbly and talkative. But as the new year began, she became angry, frustrated, and unhappy.

Erica understood that her behavior could have been in part because she was no longer the only child at home. It also may have been that she could sense her mother's anxieties. But that discernment didn't make comforting and parenting her any easier. In retrospect, Erica and I believe that this combat deployment, and my later one into the Balkans, combined with my strict military demeanor, negatively affected her more deeply than we realized at the time. The burden members of a military family, particularly children, have to bear when a parent deploys to a combat zone is great. Aggression, anger, frustration, anxiety, and depression can impact the family for years.

I know for sure that I should have been more patient and loving and less demanding when parenting our children. I had become hardened by my training and deployments, which made me very militaristic and transactional as a parent. My children were expected to do what I told them to do, and if they didn't, they got one more warning. If there was still no response to my directive, the offending child would receive a swat on her backside or a pop to the backside of her head with the palm of my hand, just like I used to get when I was growing up. There was nothing to discuss, only consequences for actions.

It was hard for me to break away from the way I was raised: primarily by my black grandmother who was raised very harshly herself during the Great Depression. She brought me up to be well mannered with no back talk at all because that was how black children were raised in her youth, stemming all the way back to her grandfather who was born a slave in America. She felt I'd have a better chance to succeed in white America if I was very obedient and a hard worker, and to some degree, she was correct—but how I translated that into my own parenting style only made it more challenging for my children to accept.

While I was in Saudi Arabia, Erica also had to become stricter with both girls, feeling that she needed to gently hold the line of discipline while being both mother *and* father to them to keep them safe, healthy, and well cared for. It was hard for Erica to carry the weight of that added responsibility while dealing with her own emotions as well as those of the girls. She did her best, and her sister certainly helped her, but Erica was never really sure if she was doing as well as she could.

I am so grateful that my family has forgiven me for my shortcomings during those tough times in our lives, and I have tried to make it up to them ever since. It is part of the price military families pay many times over as a loved one serves our country and does their part in keeping America free! Sometimes military men and women don't come back home the same person they were when they left, especially if they were in a combat situation, and some experiences change them into a person they don't want to be. I have spent the rest of my life trying to become a better person who is less aggressive and adversarial. My military training and experience made me into a rock-hard soldier with very little heart and patience for others. Sadly, that impacted how I treated my wife and children the first few years after my return. In fact, it would be another six years before I fully realized just how off track I was as a person, husband, and father.

In the end, I do not blame my upbringing, the Army, or anything else for my poor behavioral choices. I take and retain full ownership, and by the grace of God, through His Son, Jesus, I have repented of my sins and strive daily to stay in a saved relationship with Christ as my Savior. Satan has tried time and again to remind me of my sins so that I will give up on my faith and go back to my old ways. I know that there have been, and may still be, future consequences for my mistakes, but I remain in the race as the Apostle Paul stated in 1 Corinthians 9:24-27, daily fighting the good fight (2 Timothy 4:7).

My hope is to finish my race strong, but that process includes overcoming setbacks—and in early January 1991, I was under pressure, Erica was under pressure, we were a half a world apart, and it was about to get a lot worse.

My unit was prepped to enter the combat box (a military term for the area of possible enemy aggression) as part of Operation Desert Shield. We were charged with the responsibility of repairing and maintaining all Bradley fighting vehicles and missile systems, but one of my additional duties was to be in charge of the body bags if anyone in our unit was killed. It would be up to me to ensure they were properly taken care of until their bodies were shipped home for burial.

Thank God that my unit didn't sustain any casualties, but I would ultimately have to speak with more than one family during my military career about the loss of their loved one. During Operation Iraqi Freedom, one of my fellow commanders, a white, male lieutenant colonel, was killed during a combat movement. I was tasked with speaking with his mother about his service to our nation. She had been estranged from her son for many years.

She asked, "Do you think he was a good man?"

I replied with tears in my eyes, "Yes, ma'am. He was a good man who loved his country so much that he gave his last full measure of devotion to prove it."

Each one of those poignant moments have stayed with me because I knew they gave their life for me and others who served alongside them. Their sacrifice always made me tell myself, "I've got to work harder. I want to honor them by living a life of excellence and of helping others."

Essential to my well-being were the calls I made to Erica about once a week from one of the phone tents that sprung up in the combat zone. I also wrote to her every other day, and Erica usually sent faxes in response. The military did a great job getting mail and messages back and forth. The calls in particular were very comforting for Erica. They meant I was safe, I was alive, and I was talking to her. We told each other how much we loved one another. We talked about the kids' future if something happened to me. Erica gave me updates on the girls, how they were doing, and what they were up to. They told me they were praying for me. We relied on our faith. We wouldn't want to hang up.

Those communications served another, calming purpose for me. When I was with my men, I had to be Rodney Ranger. My soldiers always thought of me as being "hard as woodpecker lips," an old Army saying for someone who was hard but fair and displayed very little emotion under stress. I was also known as a leader who could overcome almost any logistical hurdle to get the job done and not complain while doing it. But when I got the faxes or phone calls from home, I didn't have to play that role. I could be a little more emotional. I truly was, and still am, such a romantic when it comes to my relationship with Erica, and such a softie with anything involving the needs of my children or grandchildren. Yet in Saudi Arabia, and later throughout my military career, all others saw was the persona that I developed to get through it. I had to lead by example at all times.

That tough guy persona was well earned. In the military, I played no less than seven Army level, or installation level, sports and won multiple championships as an individual and as part of a team. I had participated in backpack competitions, Iron Squad competitions, and Army obstacle courses and came out victorious more often than the average soldier. I was airborne, air assault, and MOUT (Military Operations on Urban Terrain) trained, a SERE (Survival, Evasion, Resistance, and Escape) instructor, and I had attended the master rappel course.

To succeed in all of these things, not to mention in a combat theater, I'd turn into a razor. I had to cut through stuff. The problem was, I wasn't always able to turn that razor off. My military service, especially in war zones, would make me edgier as a parent and as a person. I'd later see children that looked as if they had been tortured and living with next to nothing in third world countries, so I expected my children to be more appreciative for all that God was allowing me and Erica to provide them. Adding on how I grew up in poverty as an abandoned child, while my daughters were growing up with two parents in what I considered to be the lap of luxury, I could not understand why they sometimes didn't seem more aware of, or grateful for, their blessings.

I also expected them to do as they were told as if they were my soldiers. Sometimes, the way I asked my children to do things was not very loving or understanding of their needs or concerns. It was not Christlike. It was rigid and militaristic.

One thing that certainly helped take the edge off of that razor sharp persona in Saudi Arabia were the big boxes of goodies Erica began sending to me and my platoon in January. We got one every three or four weeks, and they not only contained treasured snack foods such as candy bars, suckers, gum, beef jerky, canned meats, crackers, and different cheeses, but valuable items needed in a desert environment like wet wipes, toilet paper, toothpaste, and other toiletry items. Erica's boxes became famous in our deployment zone because she drew smiley faces and wrote encouraging Bible scriptures on the outside of each one. Everyone became aware that when I received a box, I was going to share some of the items with the postal delivery person and with random soldiers near me.

> I'd turn into a razor. The problem was, I wasn't always able to turn that razor off.

Those boxes became a pivotal tool for me to spread the gospel of Jesus with my soldiers when they were on perimeter duty. I tried to go out during each around the clock shift and give the guard on duty a piece of candy or some other item to let them know how much I appreciated them and their service to our nation. When I talked with them about my faith, they responded positively. Being on guard was a scary assignment, especially at night in the desert: we were close to the enemy, and you couldn't see your hand in front of you. There was a lot of anxiety, so it was easy to talk about Christ. They had already seen enough of me to make an assessment of whether I was real or just faking it. Things had happened along the way that confirmed my faith and my concern and care for them. Of the individuals that I spoke to about God, no one ended up coming to church with me, but some did start going to our chapel.

When Desert Shield transitioned to Operation Desert Storm with the launch of air strikes on January 17, I was a platoon leader in support of the Marine force conducting combat operations directly against what we were led to believe was Saddam Hussein's elite fighting force, the famed Iraqi Republican Guard. We were loading our gear, getting ammunition, doing battle briefs, and checking vehicles. We could hear the air fighting, but I wasn't positioned to actually see them until we started traveling toward our specific operational area in the combat zone.

As our nation's attack plowed through and ultimately opened a 20-mile gap in the enemy's air defense network allowing our fighter planes, aircraft, and missiles to proceed virtually unopposed into Iraqi airspace to pummel Iraqi positions and supply lines, it felt like it was Armageddon itself—and for many Christians, there was reason to believe that may have been precisely what it was. The conflict was in the Middle East. Israel had been attacked by Hussein. It was frighteningly real, and not just for me and my fellow soldiers.

Erica had recently read Charles H. Dyer's book, *The Rise of Babylon*, popular among fundamentalist Christian believers, that claimed Hussein was in the process of rebuilding the ancient city of Babylon by regaining territory and economic power with one goal in mind: the elimination of the nation of Israel. For all the world, it looked like Dyer's speculations were proving to be prophetic, and it was genuinely scary for her to consider that I could be involved in a battle of truly biblical proportions.

Thankfully, the support of our church outside Ft. Hood helped her keep her head straight throughout it all. She received constant prayer from our pastor, his wife, and members of the congregation, many of whom were from military families of their own and could fully sympathize with the emotional and spiritual anxiety she was feeling. They helped her to see that everything described in that book was pure speculation, nothing more, and that the world wasn't coming to an end. But it was an extra factor that only raised the level of fear Erica and other military wives felt at that time.

From my perspective in combat, only God knew if we would make it back home. Gratefully, my division didn't take a lot of casualties, but we certainly contributed to causing a lot of them with our surgically effective and deadly long-range weapon systems. We moved fast across the desert. The rapid advance reminded me of the historic accounts I had read about Germany's blitzkrieg at the start of World War II. My platoon was in close support, and when one of our vehicles or missile systems were disabled, my soldiers would take them off the firing line and repair them. We were about a mile or so behind the forward edge of the battle area at any given time.

The U.S.-led coalition forces pushed through Iraqi-occupied Kuwait and into Iraq on February 24, and victory was declared after about 100 hours of ground combat. I kept a diary during those key days chronicling my harrowing experiences. I'd like to share it with you. I've chosen to retain the bad grammar, punctuation, spelling, and all to protect the realism of how it was written in the moment.

Today, 24 February 1991, is G-Day, also known as the ground invasion component for our Desert Storm battle plan. Our Airforce had been carpet bombing Iraqi targets for almost 40 days since January 17, 1991. I could hardly sleep the night before. I had major butterflies and I was wondering would I be up to the task of leading troops in combat. I prayed with my leadership team the night before G-Day and we all agreed that whatever happened we would try our best not to leave anyone on the battlefield. I know as a soldier that is what you train for daily, however, when you are actually in a combat situation it seems so surreal. This morning around 3:00 a.m. our unit was fully combat loaded and departed outpost Garcia and traveled 20 miles inside Iraq. We traveled through a breeched berm that served as our Line of Departure. This massive ground invasion was one of the largest ground invasions in Army history. We set up a perimeter that night and waited to receive our orders before we moved into direct combat with the enemy.

On day two of the ground attack phase of the war, a Bradley fighting vehicle got hit by a round from an Iraqi T-72 tank. Of the Bradley's nine-man crew, the driver was killed, and his sergeant lost his leg.

February 25, we traveled 75 more miles into occupied Iraqi territory. We had to drive our vehicles safely through unexploded munitions today. Our allied forces attacked Iraqi forces on several fronts today in Iraq and in Kuwait. Our vehicle convoy process is a very scary experience because we know we are driving through possible land mines and we have to stay in the tire tracks of the vehicles in front of you because those lanes have been cleared of land mines. If you stray off of the tire tracks in front of you, your vehicle could drive over an active land mine and cause your vehicle to set off a land mine explosion.

During our push into Iraq we passed several makeshift prisoners of war camps the allied forces had set up filled with Iraqi soldiers. Our orders were to move to contact and destroy the elite Republican Guard. Today over the radio I heard we had experienced some light casualties in our division. When someone says light casualty, what does that mean if you are that casualty? Our division's combat elements engaged the enemy and took out several of their T-72 tanks. The battlefield was lit up with M-270 Multiple Launch Rocket Systems missiles blowing up an entire grid square of one kilometer in size. We stayed up all night fixing any missile system issues with the Bradley fighting vehicles we supported.

The next day, I had to go to the charred vehicle from that engagement with the M-72 tanks and remove its operational missile system components to have them ready for use on another vehicle. I could still see the remnants of the soldiers who were killed and severely injured inside the vehicle. Dried blood stained the console, and I could still smell what seemed like burning flesh in the turret area. I noted this later in my diary when I cited the casualties of the operation.

One of those casualties was one of our attached forward support soldiers, PFC Cash. He was killed in a tank battle sometime on February 25. I met him a couple of days prior to his death while we were preparing testing his Bradley fighting vehicle missile system in the containment area prior to moving to combat. When I found out, I took a few minutes to pray for his family.

Interestingly, I didn't mention that jarring reality of war right away in my diary. Instead, I focused more broadly on what was going on around me.

February 26, I viewed a beautiful display of MLRS firepower as a Battery of MLRS's (9 systems) fired for effect into a convoy of Iraqi vehicles traveling near Basra. New orders: we were informed that the Republican Guard were retreating back towards Bagdad and our orders were to move east to cut them off and destroy as many enemies and their vehicles as we could. We drove all night toward the enemy. I could see U.S. aircraft dropping bombs in the distance and I heard artillery fire all night, it must be a living Hell for the enemy tonight.

The tank battles raged on all night the skies were lit up and the sound was deafening. We initially drove north and then east towards Kuwait. It was 4:05 a.m. February 27, I was listening to the British Broadcasting Corporation news while sitting in my Humvee vehicle in the passenger seat as my missile systems sergeant drove our vehicle. The news said that 22 divisions of the Iraqi army had surrendered. I prayed that Saddam would come to his senses and end this war by offering an unconditional surrender of his forces to the allied forces. We drove all day till we were just outside Kuwait and made camp for the night.

February 27, we began to travel closer to Kuwait along the way we passed a large Iraqi prisoner of war camp. The

Iraqi prisoners looked cold, wet, sad and hungry. I felt sorry for them and their country. We were told most of them had to join Saddam's Army or they would hurt their family members. I thanked God I was an American and I joined the Army on my own free will because I believed in America and the American Dream! We received an update from our battalion headquarters that the elite Republican Guard soldiers were trapped by allied forces between the borders of Iraq and Kuwait or what was left of them. Earlier that morning they were near the city of Basra trying to convoy back to Iraq when U.S. and allied forces aircraft bombed their convoy and killed several Iraqi soldiers and their vehicles. We were told to set up camp and to wait for further orders, maybe this was the battle that will break the back of Saddam and he will unconditionally surrender.

I witnessed the carnage on the infamous Highway of Death, the six-lane asphalt road between Kuwait and Iraq, officially known as Highway 80. Running from Kuwait City to the border town of Safwan in Iraq and then on to the Iraqi city of Basra, it was where the U.S. Air Force dropped bombs on Iraqi Army convoys, killing hundreds of retreating enemy soldiers and destroying scores of their military vehicles. As I viewed the bodies of the dead Iraqi soldiers, it made me think of what hell might look and feel like. It was a weird feeling knowing that they were real people just a few hours earlier and now were victims of a war they probably didn't even want to participate in, much less die in. My diary continued.

February 28 0800 am we were informed by the Armed Forces Network that there was a cease fire! Praise God! Is the war really over? Our mission today was to travel 70 miles southeast into Kuwait to finish off the Republican Guard unless the cease fire is for real! Our command network confirms the cease fire and AFN radio says that 29 Iraqi divisions have been rendered incapable, 25,000 Iraqi soldiers dead, 75,000 Iraqi soldiers injured, and 50,000 Iraqi POW's. Our U.S. casualties were about 200.

I poignantly concluded:

I guess the war is over, however it is still dangerous here because there are a lot of booby-trapped bunkers and unexploded munitions. We traveled by some burning munitions near some burning oil wells during our deployment. On March 2 we passed what was a battle ground a few days earlier and saw dead burnt Iraqi soldiers' bodies strewn around a bunker. I walked over to near the bunker and picked up an Iraqi soldier's knife that he would never use again.

In just those 100 hours, U.S. and allied ground forces in Iraq and Kuwait decisively defeated a battle-hardened and dangerous enemy. It may not have lasted long, but I personally saw a lot of carnage in that war. It was short and violent, my generation's war, and one that many Desert Storm veterans are still fighting on a private level due to the toxic mix of chemical warfare agents that were released during demolition operations and from spending time near Army burn pits located throughout the combat zone. Those pits were filled with items Army officials wanted to quickly discard, and the emissions from the fires have caused all kinds of medical challenges for soldiers and support personnel.

It was also discovered later that my unit was exposed to an extremely toxic nerve gas, Sarin, and many of the soldiers that I served with have become ill and died due to complications from contact with that nerve agent.

Sometimes, I still experience an event that happened to me one night during my Desert Storm close combat maintenance support operations. We had been told by headquarters that the Republican Guard were near our area of occupation. It was around midnight, and I was walking to our outermost perimeter position when someone or something started grabbing at my right leg and foot. There was a noise: it sounded like a muffled moan of pain, but I couldn't make out whether it was a human or animal because I instantly went into combat mode. I was aware of everything at once. The little details were lost in the moment. I had to operate in my peripheral senses, meaning that I may not see or know that thing that is right in front of me, but I was acutely aware of what was going on all around me.

> I personally saw a lot of carnage in that war.

I immediately kicked away whoever or whatever it was and fired my handgun in that direction. It could have been one of the wild dogs that were hungry enough to dare to come into our perimeters looking for food. It could just as well have been an enemy insurgent attempting to infiltrate our position.

Either way, I responded as I had been trained to do.

The next morning, I looked at my right leg. There were small bruises just above my right ankle near my calf muscle.

I don't know if a person or an animal was hurt or worse by my single gunshot in the desert that night. Maybe that's why I still have that dream. I always end up kicking Erica in my sleep before she wakes me up. I also have dreams at times of the charred bodies that I saw during my time in the war zone.

I can only imagine how difficult it must have been for a soldier who actually did have to fight up close and personal in the Civil War, World Wars I and II, or any other close combat war, who then came home and was expected to live a normal life like nothing ever happened. There is a reason so many soldiers come back from combat and commit suicide.

After I retired from the Army, I received some professional psychological assistance to help me process my combat experiences in a way that allowed me to function as a productive citizen. Contrary to what some believe, it is not a sign of weakness to seek psychiatric care. It takes a real man or woman to ask for mental help when they need it. Nevertheless, when I worked years later for the Huntsville Police Department as a communications relations officer, I had to witness or report on several occasions about people (adults and children) who were injured or traumatized. It got to the point that I had to leave that job so that I wouldn't have to continue seeing the trauma of others while still dealing with my own trauma that carried over from my service during Desert Storm.

Since my wartime experience in Iraq, I wear hearing aids because of the noise of the shelling as I worked near the missile systems. I've also had to undergo no less than 35 different surgeries. All my major joints have been operated on. I was also diagnosed with severe sleep apnea (I was given what was, at that time, the only sleep apnea device approved by the Federal Food and Drug Administration and had it implanted in my chest to keep my airway open at night), chronic fatigue, severe skin irritations, and post-traumatic stress disorder—all as a result of my brief time in combat.

Such combined symptoms were given a name sometime shortly after the war ended: Gulf War Syndrome. It's all treatable, and I'm not complaining. I thank God that my health has stabilized, and the Veterans Administration (VA) has been good to me, providing the myriad of medical services and tracking the many surgeries and ailments I continue to experience, so I can live a productive life. It's a reality for me that I know is not always the case for every sick or injured military man or woman.

Still, after my comrades started to die from the mysterious side effects of Gulf War Syndrome, I felt survivor's guilt since I have lived so much longer than most of the other men and women that served in the same battle areas that I did during Desert Storm. Yet that has made me more determined to live my life to the fullest to honor the memory of my fallen comrades.

I have often heard the debate about whether or not Operation Desert Storm was a war the U.S. should have entered. I feel that we saved lives that, without our presence in the region, may have otherwise been lost. We were able to drive Iraqi forces out of Kuwait, and we stabilized the area. We did our part, and I am proud to have been a part of it.

In May 1991, after five months in the Middle East, my troops and I boarded a commercial airliner in Saudi Arabia for the flight back to Germany. I was in uniform on the civilian flight sitting in coach seats when a stewardess asked me to follow her. I got up, she led me to the first class section, and told me to have a seat. It was one of the last flights for me and other members of my unit who hadn't already returned to Germany.

I didn't feel the least bit guilty about sitting in first class for the first time in my life. I was blessed to have been honored with the opportunity to do so. I was relieved. I was proud of my performance under fire. I learned a lot about myself in leadership, and I was even presented with the Bronze Star, given to military men and women from all branches of the military for meritorious service, combat action, or both, before leaving Saudi Arabia.

Yet I was sad at seeing so much death. It was the first time that I had really seen the reality of war up close. It did not lessen how gung-ho I was about being an Army soldier and leader. I was more appreciative of life in general. But in some ways, it contributed to my hardness around Erica and the girls because I expected more.

More out of myself.

More appreciation from my children.

More from my soldiers. People died, and I needed to train my soldiers as hard as I could. I didn't want any of them to be one of those who didn't pay attention or follow safety requirements and became a casualty of war. That officer who died in Operation Iraqi Freedom was lost because someone in his convoy did not adhere to safety issues during their convoy operation. Somebody didn't do something right, and he died as a result.

I would never accept that happening to anyone under my charge.

Erica and the girls finally joined me in Germany in June 1991. Upon my return from combat, I had secured family housing quarters for us in Hösbach, Germany in a government leased housing unit in a beautiful countryside location. We got a modern, German-style condominium on the second floor of the unit. It had a spacious balcony overlooking a garden of trees, shrubs peppered with little yellow flowers, and beautiful petunias and geraniums in full bloom. It was so lush and green. The condo itself had three bedrooms, new appliances, an open concept kitchen, and a launderette in the basement. An extra storage area inside our garage, as well as an attic, provided ample storage for my Army field gear. Many of our neighbors had windows adorned with flower boxes. It was like living in a villa at Disney World.

Erica then began what became a decade-long career as a dental assistant by attending training in nearby Hanau, Germany through a military spouse grant. There was a shortage of dental technicians and hygienists, and it gave her work while we were stationed there and a marketable skill that she could take to the States with her. We once again attended the International Church of God of Prophecy in Langen where I shared a few words from the pulpit thanking the congregation for their prayers, and for checking on my family while I was away in the war zone.

Still, it was very difficult to go back to being a husband, father, and peacetime soldier after being in Saudi Arabia. After my war zone experience, normal life was somewhat of a letdown. I was used to being on full alert and commanding my troops to be prepared to meet the enemy. I was on edge for many months after my return, my parenting style became even more demanding, and I was sometimes short with Erica as well.

As I received orders for us to return to the United States in June 1992, I was especially excited about the new assignment. It was at Ft. Rucker in southern Alabama near the city of Dothan. I had been chosen to become a TAC officer and one of the new generation of "Black Hats" officers: those who wore black baseball caps to denote who they were. My specific task was to train enlisted soldiers to become brand new warrant officer candidates.

At age 32, the Army was trusting me to train the next generation, and I saw it as validation. After all, it was well recognized that only the best of the best warrant officers were assigned as TAC officers due to the amount of influence and power they would hold over the warrant officer candidates during training and throughout their careers as potential mentors. The Army Aviation Command Deputy Commanding General later saw me in person and said I was the best TAC "bar none." His comment using that old military term is even in the official Army records, and it would lead to numerous other opportunities throughout the rest of my career.

When we arrived at Ft. Rucker, military housing was waiting for us: a roomy one-level ranch-style home with a front and back yard and a carport in a nice neighborhood with other officers and their families on the installation. One month after we arrived, I was also ordained by the Church of God of Prophecy national leadership as a deacon, the first of several ministry positions I'd hold in the denomination in the years ahead. Our new congregation was located in nearby Elba, Alabama, and my position there showed that anyone could be in ministry for the Lord if they were willing to work, in good faith, on their personal shortcomings.

We could have attended a more established Church of God of Prophecy location, but Erica told me that God spoke to her heart to tell us to go to Elba, an economically depressed area, instead of a more diverse and affluent church. Positioned in a flood zone, the majority of the church's families depended on welfare checks for their survival. I could definitely relate to their plight. The attendees were all white, and many of them had grown up with parents who were prejudiced against people of color.

Erica and I thrived at the church. Almost every week, we taught Sunday school to the kids as husband and wife, often taking them out to lunch afterward before returning to church to play different sports. Erica also taught the children about self-care, personal grooming, and dental care, and we took the kids camping several times which allowed them to gain confidence in themselves and deepen their growing faith in Christ.

At work, I still had to be a tough officer as I trained enlisted soldiers and some civilians. While I was strict, I found myself softening, even when I didn't necessarily have to, because I didn't want my cadets to hate me. Although I played the role by hollering, threatening, and taking stuff away when needed to instill discipline, I tried to do it all with love and professionalism. I was determined not to be an egotistical jerk like some of the other TAC officers I worked with. I always warned someone before I turned them in for disciplinary measures, ensuring that I had observed their unacceptable behavior correctly and, in some cases, giving them a chance to correct their behavior. Sadly, I had to turn in a couple of my coworkers for being tyrants and even racists because they had so much power. We truly wielded life and death over somebody's career, including where they went and how much money they made. Other officers displayed this authority with a flippant comment or wave of the hand. I tried to be more caring.

> While I was strict, I found myself softening, even when I didn't necessarily have to.

In addition, I got into the best shape of my life at Ft. Rucker and honed my leadership skills in ways that I never thought I could, particularly while teaching survival skills. One of the candidates I trained during my two years as a TAC officer at Ft. Rucker contacted me many years later to thank me for teaching him the survival skills he needed as an Army aviator when he was shot down over Iraq. I was so humbled and overwhelmed by his gratitude.

During my third year at Ft. Rucker, I was the first warrant officer selected to participate in the pilot Warrant Officer Degree Completion program, and I went to school for a full year to complete my bachelor's degree at Troy State University in Dothan. While I was in college, I was able to take my family to Disney World for a week. It was one of the most wonderful times we'd ever had together as a family. By then, our youngest daughter was five and our oldest daughter was 13, and we took a 10-year-old nephew from my wife's side of the family along with us. We often look at the photos of that trip and remember how much fun we had.

Finally, the assignment to Ft. Rucker gave me many opportunities to see my son again. He was a teenager, and I was hoping the renewed interaction would be a good thing for our blended family—but it was not. He was beginning to mature into a young man, and he had all kinds of issues. With each new visit, we noticed him becoming more aggressive. He had gotten into hip hop music and the sometime thug lifestyle associated with it. He was smoking marijuana, getting into trouble at school for bad conduct, and behind in all of his classes. He had been suspended for fighting and threatening fellow students and teachers.

As we spent time with him, sometimes for days at a time, Erica and I tried to guide him to make better life choices, but it became apparent that he was on a track we could not derail him from. It was a shame he couldn't make that Disney World trip with us. Who knows how things may have turned out later if he had been able to have that special time with us.

Even the smallest events can change a person forever.

When I received orders to go back to Germany in June 1995, Erica and I were more than a little sad about it because of the relationship we were trying to rebuild with my son, but my reputation as a trainer and leader had blossomed. I realized I was truly making a strategic difference in the Army that would continue to pay dividends for years to come. Plus, for the first time, we were going to be able to fly overseas together as a family. My unit had also assigned me a sponsor that had already put us on the list for senior officer family quarters.

When we arrived at Miesau Army Depot near Landstuhl, Germany, our quarters were ready and waiting, and I was the senior missile systems officer overseeing a platoon of 50 soldiers. I was also the leader for the ground support platoon responsible for repairing all of the various missile systems, generators, batteries, and night sight systems. One of my primary duties was to ensure all direct and general support maintenance was performed on all pre-positioned missile systems across the military European theater. I traveled all over Europe to places like Amsterdam, Luxemburg, Belgium, Bavaria, and France.

It was extra special, thinking back to that kid who couldn't have imagined traveling anywhere, to go to all of those places in a position of authority. Whenever I arrived, people were "hopping and popping" (coming to attention and delivering a crisp salute). I'd come home from trips and say to Erica, "Honey, they are trusting me with this stuff. It is unbelievable!"

I'd certainly come a long way from my first travel "assignment" when I'd first arrived in Germany as a green behind the ears 20 year old. That's when I was directed to transport a convicted drug addict across that country to take him to the big

Army jail in Mannheim. I got lost and turned around four or five times. It was a miracle I got the guy to prison, much less found my way back to the base.

My military career was going great—but behind the scenes, I was just trying to keep it together. By the fall of 1995, I had been married for almost 15 years to an incredible wife. I had a 17-year-old son apart from her and two wonderful daughters with her who were 14 and six years old. A lot of happiness was mixed with trauma, sadness, and lingering hurt from the past.

Harry Hobbs was still very much a work in progress, and a massive personal crossroads was still ahead.

Chapter 8

THE FLAWS HIT HOME

According to a report by the U.S. Army's chief of military history, Bosnia-Herzegovina was the scene for the most violent armed conflict in Europe since World War II. Four of the six republics—Slovenia, Croatia, Bosnia-Herzegovina, and Macedonia—separated from Yugoslavia between 1991 and 1992. Each secession was contested, with the most horrific destruction and violence occurring in Bosnia-Herzegovina. At least half of the entire population—more than two million people—was directly affected by a civil war that lasted from April 1992 to November 1995.

A peace agreement was signed in December 1995 authorizing the North Atlantic Treaty Organization (NATO) to intervene. The NATO Implementation Force, consisting of 60,000 military personnel, one-third of them American, was created to enforce the peace and to facilitate the reconstruction of the country. A total of three successive peace enforcement operations were undertaken: Joint Endeavor, Joint Guard, and Joint Forge.

My second deployment into a combat zone came that same month to Kaposvár, Hungary where I was assigned to the Five Hundred Sixty-Third Ordnance Company in support of

Operation Joint Endeavor under the flag of the Twenty-Ninth Support Group. Located at Taszár Air Base, a small, old base east of Kaposvár, my company's primary mission was to execute the reception, staging, and onward movement and integration (RSOI) of troops and equipment into Bosnia-Herzegovina.

As we prepared to operate the RSOI, I started out as a backup to the backup officer in charge of railhead operations. This operation was designed to ensure that all Army equipment was safely tied down on railcar beds and then successfully transported to its destination to be untied and safely offloaded for combat operations. It also entailed safe passage of all necessary Army personnel on those trains. During our pre-deployment briefing, I remember thinking that at least I wouldn't be in charge like I was in Saudi Arabia and would have a more senior officer to follow and support.

Little did I know then that the officers ahead of me would eventually be relieved by the battalion commander because they lacked the necessary leadership qualities and were unable to get the work done properly to prepare to run the RSOI correctly.

In less than two weeks, I became the railhead officer in charge of the largest RSOI in Europe since the second world war.

My philosophy had always been to keep my head in the game because you never know when you'll get a chance to step up and shine. I had often said to my leaders, "I may not have been your first choice, but once you give me a chance, I'll show you that I'm your best choice."

Once more, my chance had come. But could I prove myself capable of leading this critical combat operation?

That night, I went to my sleeping quarters, got on my knees, and prayed for the strength, knowledge, and leadership to do what I needed to do. I felt like David must've felt when he asked

God to help him prior to going into combat in Psalm 59:1-2. He cried, "Deliver me from my enemies, O God; be my fortress against those who are attacking me. Deliver me from evildoers and save me from those who are after my blood."

About a week later, I had to provide a briefing of my RSOI plan to all of the combat generals in the theater of operation on how I was going to lead over 200 soldiers to perform in one of the most dangerous operations the Army conducts outside of actual combat. It was by far the biggest moment, and the most important group I had ever spoken before, in my career. It took place at a large civic auditorium in Taszár. I was driven there by soldiers who would normally be escorting more senior field grade officers, not a junior officer like me. It was a little overwhelming. I felt like a rock star preparing to sing at a large concert. I arrived early and was the most nervous I had ever been in my life.

The second person on the agenda to give a briefing, I took the stage and provided an overview of how my railhead teams would safely download the incoming equipment, vehicles, and personnel. Several of the general officers present asked questions concerning logistics, command, and control, and I replied with confidence and professionalism to the combat commanders. The supreme allied commander was one of the generals in attendance. I couldn't believe God had allowed me to speak on such a grand stage. My briefing was well received, and my battalion commander told me he was proud of the way I stepped up to take on the challenge of being the railhead officer in charge. Back in my room that evening, I was very thankful the briefing went well and that all the generals were supportive and approved of my plans to conduct the railhead operation safely.

For the RSOI, I was given a driver and two Hungarian interpreters to help me communicate with the railroad authorities.

I continued feeling like a rock star until the responsibility on my shoulders and the work ahead brought me back to reality. Among other things, it was my job to ensure that all personnel that arrived at the railhead were fed and issued ammunition, equipment, and vehicles before they loaded up and went to their combat positions. I was also responsible for the health, welfare, and safety of two railhead teams of 100 soldiers each that conducted unending railhead operations in winter conditions and temperatures that dropped to 20 degrees below zero for three consecutive weeks. I got frost bite on two of my fingers during the operation, and they still burn today whenever I am in cold weather.

Each day, I ran the A shift from 6:00 a.m. until 6:00 p.m. The B shift was run by a lieutenant from 6:00 p.m. to 6:00 a.m., and I often checked in on them around midnight to ensure they had the resources they needed to accomplish their mission. Each shift safely downloaded all soldiers, equipment, vehicles, and weapon systems. They provided meals for the soldiers, and if needed, they also administered medical attention before the soldiers traveled to their areas of occupation as directed by their combat commanders. Over a two month-plus period from December 15 to February 20, my team and I supervised the downloading of 165 trains, 3,750 railcars, 5,500 pieces of equipment, and 650 military vans.

By the grace of God, and through the hard work of all of my soldiers, the RSOI went great except for one incident that was out of my control or oversight. A soldier died when he was electrocuted during the deployment train trip in a small town before arriving at the Taszár railhead. When the officer in charge gave me the bad news, I made sure the rest of the soldiers on that train were taken care of, and I asked the military chaplains to come and speak with any soldier who was in need of emotional support due to the tragedy.

As a result of my dedication and perseverance, zero accidents were reported under my supervision and guidance. Late in the deployment, the Army secretary of defense and the supreme allied commander visited the railhead to congratulate me and my team for developing new Army doctrine for establishing railhead operations on the RSOI. My leadership ability had drawn a lot of attention.

They were also there to present coins that all key Army leaders give to military members or civilians who they feel have gone above and beyond to perform their duties at a high level or who have done something extraordinary to allow others to accomplish their missions. The coins I received, emblazoned with shields, swords, and flags, were normally presented to officers of higher rank. They were larger, more colorful, and held more prestige than other military coins, and included several engraved from the Joint Chiefs of Staff and one embossed by General Colin L. Powell himself. The amount that was given so quickly was overwhelming, and I'm blessed to say that I have been fortunate enough to have received over 125 such coins during and after my military career.

During the nearly four months I was deployed, Erica and I stayed in touch by satellite phone at least once a week. As always, she was my constant support and motivation, and she did all the usual heavy lifting for our family in raising our children and taking care of our home. Her typical day consisted of preparing breakfast for our oldest daughter and making sure she was fed, clean, dressed, and ready to go off to school before touching up the house, awakening our toddler, and cleaning, dressing, and feeding her. While she played, Erica continued to take care of our home by cleaning bathrooms, fixing beds, doing laundry on wash days, sweeping, and mopping and ironing when needed, as well as scheduling appointments or taking the little one with her to run errands. Erica made sure to take time out to play with our toddler, change diapers and familiarize her with the potty, prepare snacks and food for her, and read, sing, and do crafts with her before planning dinner. During nap time, she usually took advantage of the opportunity to read and study the Bible or other books.

When our older daughter returned home from school each day, they'd have snacks, rest, and play just a little before homework. After homework was done, it was time for dinner, after which our oldest played with her sister or her friends or did some reading. After dinner clean up, they'd usually do something special together—like write a note or make a craft to include in a package they sent to me almost every other week, watch a movie, or go outside to play or swim—before preparing everyone for bed, culminating with a story, prayers, kisses, and hugs goodnight.

Erica was amazing.

I returned from Operation Joint Endeavor to my unit in Germany at the end of February 1996. My success led to me being chosen as a commercial spokesperson for the Army in Europe. They showcased video recordings of me leading troops off the train when they arrived at the railhead and discussing safety. I was also interviewed by CNN, and I was on a series of European television commercials. This role was what prepared me for my later stint as a spokesperson for the Huntsville Police Department, as well as for the city's utility company.

In March of that year, my family and I were asked to perform in our military community church Easter play sponsored by the Army Chapel on Landstuhl Kaserne. It was called, "The Silence is Broken," and it focused on Jesus rising from the dead and ascending to the right hand of the Father. Appropriately, I played a soldier: the Roman centurion who was at the cross of the crucifixion. Erica was a stagehand and helped with scene changes while our daughters participated as two young Jewish girls in the market scene.

This experience helped to heal and bond our family after my return from my second time in a war zone. I was still a little distant, and the experience allowed me to fully reintegrate back into a normal, everyday interaction with Erica and the girls. One of the hardest things for a soldier returning from deployment, especially from a combat zone, is adjusting to how the family operates. It is never quite the same as before deployment because both the soldier and family have changed.

Erica was amazing.

Another challenge for me with that reintegration was that my mother's health had started to deteriorate. I made an official request to the Department of the Army for compassionate reassignment to allow me to return to stateside duty prior to completing my full tour in Germany. The Army quickly approved my request and reassigned me to Ft. Campbell, Kentucky where there was a slot available for a missile systems officer.

Such reassignment is only approved if a close family member is determined by a medical professional to be terminal within one year. That was the case for my momma.

We returned to the United States, and I was assigned to the Eight Hundred First Maintenance Support Battalion supporting the One Hundred First Airborne Division. We briefly lived in temporary lodging in an apartment complex located on post before being given a three-bedroom ranch style house on Ft. Campbell and settling ourselves in for our new tour of duty. It would see me recognized for implementing my unit's first program to ensure that all missile float systems were always fully operational. A missile float system is an extra, unassigned missile system that can quickly replace an existing missile system that needs preventative maintenance or is waiting for an inoperative part on order. We had three missile float systems that were always maintained so our missile fleet could be at 100 percent at all times. This program saved the Army thousands of dollars and increased readiness rates for our division.

Ultimately, my high level of expertise, experience, and responsibility resulted in me being named fleet manager of the division's material management center. It supplied over 30 fleets of equipment— vehicles, missile systems, and rolling stock such as trailers or vans—for the division's support command. I was the first missile maintenance warrant officer recognized for having the highest fleet readiness in the recent history of the division.

As a family, we were able to spend quality time visiting my mother at her nursing home in Louisville for about a year before she passed away in the fall of 1997. This included many trips there with both of our daughters, and she was very proud of my military accomplishments. That meant so much to me because I felt like I was keeping the promise I made to her years earlier when I told her that I would become one of the best soldiers in Army history. The last time we visited was a few days before she died. In her room, she went in and out of consciousness a couple of times but, at one point, became very lucid and spoke clearly while looking deeply into my eyes. She told me how much she loved us and how proud she was of me and my family.

I will always cherish that moment and her kind words. Despite the circumstances of my birth, I will always appreciate that momma never treated me with anything but love and respect. When she was not sick or having a mental episode, momma was one of the most loving people I have ever known.

Right after her death, my family went through a crucible that almost broke us. Before our arrival at Ft. Campbell, Erica had decided that she wanted to be a stay-at-home mom. God made it clear in her heart and mind that she needed to continue to be available for our girls. However, our oldest daughter and I strongly encouraged her to continue using the dental skills that she had worked so hard to obtain and remain working, at least on a part time basis. We told Erica that we would work together to ensure our youngest daughter would be taken care of when Erica was at work.

My wife knew that was not her calling from God, but she reluctantly and unwisely decided to follow the advice we gave her instead, and she began working again. Before long, she was enjoying her work so much that it started to take up time that she feels she should have been spending with our family and using to take better care of the girls.

Even though my oldest daughter and I thought it was the best decision, Erica was fully aware it was not God's will. The Bible addresses these situations directly. Four passages come to mind. "Do not conform to the pattern of this world, but be transformed by the renewing of your mind. Then you will be able to test and approve what God's will is—his good, pleasing and perfect will." (Romans 12:2) "Whatever you do, work at it with all your heart, as working for the Lord, not for human masters." (Colossians 3:23) "Am I now trying to win the approval of human beings, or of God? Or am I trying to please people? If I were still trying to please people, I would not be a servant of Christ." (Galatians 1:10) Finally, "We must obey God rather than human beings!" (Acts 5:29)

As Erica was returning to work, I was selfishly playing several Army sports while taking graduate level college courses in the evenings. Even worse, our younger daughter was starting to believe that we were not a healthy family unit. I won't share details of her experiences, but they were traumatic. She was passed around between the three of us during this very critical time in her life. I had placed responsibility beyond what she was able to handle to help watch her sister. During this season, the four of us did very little together as a family. We didn't take the time to enjoy each other, and it weighed heavily on our daughters and on our relationship as a couple.

I take the blame for all of that as the husband and head of our household. I was caught up with winning trophies and getting pats on the back. I had truly bought into the world's ethos of being number one at everything, but I was not using that same energy to ensure my family was taken care of at all times.

I was living the familiar Army motto, "Be all that you can be." However, I was not doing what was needed for my family to be all that it could be.

We were out of balance.

We needed help and prayer to survive.

First, Erica and I both fasted and prayed for clear direction from God on how our family should proceed. Our pastor had been preaching from Mark 9:29 and saying that tough challenges in life can only be overcome by praying and fasting together. With this in mind, Erica and I went on a 30-day prayer and intermediate fast (meaning we ate one to two small meals a day) to hear from God about the changes our family needed to make to flourish and become healthy.

During this month-long period, I'd wake up at 4:00 a.m. each day to train for an Army Iron Man competition that was coming up. Even though we were fasting, I had the stamina to do it. One morning, after drinking my protein shake, I left the house with a 60-pound ruck sack on my back to begin a five mile run. About one mile in, a realization hit me: I had been running from my responsibilities as a husband and father, in part through taking the time and effort to participate in Army competitions, seven different sports, and attending college at night.

I was once again prioritizing my needs and my career over my family—and we had reached the limit of what we could endure and stay together. The convicting truth of Mark 8:36-37 echoed in my mind and permeated my spirit. "What good is it for someone to gain the whole world, yet forfeit their soul? Or what can anyone give in exchange for their soul?" The context of the revelation was clear.

I was nearing close to 20 years of Army service, and I had been offered a job as a high school instructor by the Army Junior Reserve Officer Training Corps. Should I retire and support my wife's dental career? Should I stay in the Army and go to the top? Should Erica stop working and ensure our youngest daughter was properly taken care of? Decisions had to be made.

In addition to fasting and praying, my oldest daughter and I received Christian counseling from our church pastor to help us learn to interact better. We had drifted apart over the years and discovered that we were not in sync. We were not communicating as we should, and our relationship was deteriorating. The counseling gave us the tools to help rectify that.

In addition, Erica and I agreed that she would no longer pursue a career in the dental field, and we chose a date for her to terminate her job so that she could be home with our daughters. We decided, too, that I would continue my Army career and push for 30 years because we had not yet met our long-term financial goals—but I was going to start better considering my family and their needs and feelings whenever I took an assignment or considered volunteering for training.

Personally, I made a real change in my thinking concerning my family responsibilities, and I prioritized increased quiet time with God and individual prayer time with Him. I was determined to be a more patient father and husband, with the understanding that it was going to be a slow process. I began to speak softer and more patiently with my family. I accepted that it wasn't going to be the challenges themselves that we'd remember later in life, but how we addressed them and communicated with each other as we dealt with them. I strived to become more respectful, empathetic, and sympathetic.

I realized I was broken. I was seared from being a soldier and a razor. I had to truly change.

By God's grace, our family weathered the storm. I could have handled it much better than I did, but I believed it was up to me, the man of God in our home, to lead my family at all times: good, bad, and everything in between. We also decided as a family to start being more considerate of each other and to work together more often, and I began looking for opportunities in the community to allow us to practice and demonstrate that process.

That summer, my family and I answered an open audition for anyone who wanted to be in a major community play of The Wizard of Oz. Our oldest daughter, like her mother, had a wonderful singing voice. She went out for, and was given, the role of Dorothy, winning it over 30 other girls, some of whom had been formally trained vocally and others who had been community actors or professional dancers in previous community performances. She became the first brown skinned person ever to be given that role in that community play.

Our youngest girl was offered the Mayor of Munchkin City, but she turned it down because she didn't want a male part. She was cast as one of the Lullaby League ballerina munchkins instead. Erica preferred to stay behind the scenes, volunteering to work with the kids and to help them change costumes between scenes.

I believed I could reprise the part of the Tin Man that I had played back in high school. Though I didn't get the role, I was chosen as the understudy. That ended up being a big blessing because it gave me more time to practice lines with my oldest daughter.

> I was seared from being a soldier and a razor. I had to truly change.

It was a wonderful bonding time for us. We attended hours of practice, and our oldest daughter was assigned a professional voice coach for the final weeks prior to the play. On opening night, the community theater was full, and our Dorothy was awesome! She received a standing ovation at the close of each of the three showings of the play, and the military newspaper at Ft. Campbell highlighted our girls in an article about the performance. Thanks to that experience, The Wizard of Oz will always hold a special place in our family's hearts and minds. It was a healing and cathartic season for all of us, and Erica and I could not have been prouder of our daughters.

In fall 1998, our oldest daughter began her senior year of high school and decided that she wanted to join the U.S. Air Force upon graduation. I also received orders to be reassigned to Ft. Rucker in Alabama as a senior instructor for all warrant officers in leadership training. My report date was July 1999, and our oldest daughter joined the Air Force a few days before we left Ft. Campbell. She and I had come a long way together by then, and I was very proud of her for deciding to serve our country at about the same age I did. I was excited that she would get to see the world and have a chance to find out who she was without the constraints of my authoritative parenting style. Knowing that she was going into the military during peace time, so there was no concern about her safety, Erica was relieved. She also believed the structured environment would have a positive effect on her as she entered her early adult years.

As we drove away from Ft. Campbell, I was proud that I had completed my master's degree and obtained my first doctorate degree while I was there. I was also well aware and grateful for all that we had been through and everything we had survived as a family during that time.

Back at Ft. Rucker, I went to work as the first missile system maintenance warrant officer assigned to the Warrant Officer Career College as the staff course manager. This was a supreme honor, and I trained thousands of warrant officers in ethics,

Army leadership doctrine, and how the Army operates, allowing them to benefit from my growing management and leadership skills. That opportunity made me the only warrant officer to date in Army history to have taught every level of warrant officer training.

Erica and I also returned to the Church of God of Prophecy in Elba to resume our previous work there with the underprivileged children in that congregation and community. We developed strong relationships at the church, especially with the kids. In addition, we taught the children there how to develop a better work ethic and raise money. That resulted in the construction of a new youth wing on the church's property. The funds were donated by the Non-Commissioned Officers Academy at Ft. Rucker after we shared the need with military leaders there.

During the week, I trained the Army's senior warrant officers. Over the weekends, I often preached at the church as associate pastor and youth ministry leader. One of my most special experiences at the church came when I was able to baptize my youngest daughter in a ceremony we had for the youth group. The baptism took place on a bright, sunny day in summer 2000 at a public pool near the home of one of the church members. Prior to the ceremony, my daughter and I studied scriptures on baptism such as Matthew 28:19-20. "Therefore go and make disciples of all nations, baptizing them in the name of the Father and of the Son and of the Holy Spirit, and teaching them to obey everything I have commanded you. And surely I am with you always, to the very end of the age."

The pastor allowed me and my daughter to go first. We got into the pool, and I read aloud the Apostle Peter's words in Acts 2:38-39. "Repent and be baptized, every one of you, in the name of Jesus Christ for the forgiveness of your sins. And you will receive the gift of the Holy Spirit. The promise is for you and your children and for all who are far off—for all whom the Lord our God will call." Then she waded over to me, I gave her a hug, and I told her how much I loved her before declaring, "I now baptize you in the name of the Father, the Son, and the Holy Ghost."

We had talked about her putting her fingers over her nose when I dipped her down. She smiled, I lowered her into the water, and then raised her up. As she rubbed the water out of her eyes, she said she loved me before departing the pool. It was an emotional moment, but I managed to get myself together to stay and assist the pastor as he baptized the rest of the kids in line.

It was an awesome and humbling experience to baptize my own daughter. It was the first of many experiences and opportunities that allowed me to grow closer to her. Those experiences made me wish that I had bonded more often with my oldest girl before she grew up and left home, but I was grateful for my moments with her, whether in The Wizard of Oz or during our appearance together in "The Silence is Broken." During the final scene, when the crucifixion was portrayed, my oldest daughter came over and stood beside me. I felt so humbled to be standing near her and thinking about how everyone has a chance at redemption as long as there is breath in our bodies.

When I wasn't at work, I was able to move away from being a hard core soldier, particularly as Erica and I worked with the underprivileged children at our church. Sometimes I had to get tough, telling them to stop feeling sorry for themselves because they were living in poverty and broken homes. I had been where they were. I encouraged the kids by telling them that they were okay and to pick themselves up. We taught them personal hygiene, took them camping, and sought to give them experiences and insights they'd never get otherwise.

We mentored many who did not have parents in their lives, and God used my personal experience as a biracial person to help teach the white youth at our church that the racism they may have been taught was wrong in the eyes of Jesus. Many of those youth have kept in contact with us over the years, and several went on to marry people of color.

It was a wonderful time in my life. I was starting to move past the angst I carried with me from my two combat deployments.

Then came the shock of September 11, 2001. I was settling into my morning routine teaching the senior warrant officers in my designated classroom when text messages started flooding my phone. Busy at the moment, I told myself I would check them during the next class break. A few minutes later, one of my fellow instructors walked into my classroom.

"Give the class an early 10-minute break," he said. "I need to inform you of something."

I dismissed the officers, and he delivered the news. "America is under attack by suicide terrorists that highjacked four American airliners."

I then checked the texts. Many of my Army friends stationed all over the world had messaged me about the attacks. On the news, I learned that two of the planes had crashed into the twin towers of the World Trade Center in New York City. I went straight to my commander's office. One warrant officer was speaking with another senior warrant officer stationed at The Pentagon when, all of a sudden, there was a loud sound, and the call was cut off. At that moment, another plane crashed into The Pentagon.

As I watched the footage of the attacks on the television, I tried to imagine what I would've been like if Erica or one of my daughters had been on one of those aircraft and how I would have felt to see them perish that way. It was unbelievable and horrible to see everything play out in real time on TV. As an Army officer, however, those feelings were punctuated by anger. I was ready at that moment to go back to war to defend our freedoms after the unprovoked attack on U.S. soil. It didn't matter that I had already been to two other war zones. If the Army needed my skill set to help fight this new global war on terror, I was eager to serve. Over the next few weeks, the Army made plans for how it would respond to this heinous act of terror. It didn't fully deploy to retaliate against the attacks until 2003. In the meantime, about six months after 9-11, I received orders to report to Ft. Sill in Oklahoma to become a detachment commander.

It was a full circle moment. I had completed basic training at Ft. Sill in 1978, and now I was returning as the first missile systems maintenance warrant officer to be hand selected as a training detachment commander, the Army's only operational Army warrant officer commander position, at the Army's sole radar repair school. It felt like I had been preparing for that position my entire Army career. I saw little Harry saluting as a Boy Scout, so rigid and such a little soldier. I had always wanted to be in charge and lead from the front, and my opportunity had finally come.

As detachment commander, I was responsible for overseeing multiple levels of radar training for thousands of U.S. Army and Marine soldiers and officers, as well as all allied forces. The Marines even gave me a uniform with my name on it. I was in charge of a team of instructors as they prepared the soldiers to be technical experts, ensuring that future combat commanders were provided competent maintenance workers on the battle-field. I realized how important it was for me to ensure that all of my military and civilian radar instructors were at the top of their game with knowledge and techniques to impart to our U.S. military members and allies now that the post-September 11, 2001 War on Terror was underway.

As usual, Erica and I were on the Army housing list, but we had been told it could be a year before permanent quarters would be available. So, we moved into temporary housing while we searched for a home to rent in the city of Lawton, Oklahoma. As we drove through different neighborhoods looking for a house, we went into a predominately African American, lower income area and came up to a home located at 2610 NW Twenty-Sixth Street.

Right then, God revealed to me that we should rent that home and start a ministry there to share the Gospel with the underprivileged children in that community. When our realtor informed us that the home had previously been owned by a drug dealer and that the crime rate was high in the neighborhood, I was concerned about my family's safety, but I knew God was speaking to me. I had to listen and be His servant.

We rented the home, and I wouldn't have traded that ministry opportunity for anything. Our local church, First Church of God (there wasn't a Church of God of Prophecy nearby), provided a bus so that Erica and I could transport neighborhood children to church on Sundays and for other special services.

> I knew God was speaking to me. I had to listen and be His servant.

Other young military couples sometimes accompanied us to help with the children, and members of the women's Bible study group that Erica attended graciously donated leftover Sunday School materials and snacks for our youth ministry.

But that wasn't all. The police department worked with us to form a neighborhood watch group in that community, and representatives from the Lawton city council partnered with us to run a Drug Education For Youth Camp for underprivileged youths living in high-risk areas in the town. We prayed about this educational opportunity, and God gave us permission to move forward. I secured the required permission from the Army to lead the event, and Erica organized the camp. We recruited a team of trusted adults, mostly young soldiers, to assist us. We managed a $10,000 budget, a volunteer work force of 20 adults, and over 40 campers. The camp experience and the training we delivered helped many of the youth who attended to make better decisions about drug use, and it built up their self-esteem as well as their fitness and nutrition habits.

My detachment commander duties for 30 active-duty soldiers and 11 civilians came with a variety of challenges, including dealing with an instructor who was a practicing Satanist. His wife, also one my instructors, was an active Wiccan. When I took command and noticed that some of my instructors were not conducting themselves as professionally as they should in the classroom, I instituted processes and procedures to ensure they became more knowledgeable and increased their accountability when teaching their students.

Nevertheless, it became apparent to me that students were being distracted by the Satanist instructor because he was trying to recruit them to join his religion. Therefore, I had to remove him from his job. I later learned that he and his wife had placed a hex on me after I processed him out of the Army. Apparently,

Wiccan followers were prevalent in that region of the country in the early 2000s.

Erica and I prayed that God would help us display the right attributes to conduct ourselves with godly character, and to reflect the love and truth of Jesus Christ, throughout the bizarre situation. We were inspired by two passages of Scripture, the first from 1 Peter 5:8. "Be alert and of sober mind. Your enemy the devil prowls around like a roaring lion looking for someone to devour." The second was found in Isaiah 6:5-8. "'Woe to me!' I cried. 'I am ruined! For I am a man of unclean lips, and I live among a people of unclean lips, and my eyes have seen the King, the Lord Almighty.' Then one of the seraphim flew to me with a live coal in his hand, which he had taken with tongs from the altar. With it he touched my mouth and said, 'See, this has touched your lips; your guilt is taken away and your sin atoned for.' Then I heard the voice of the Lord saying, 'Whom shall I send? And who will go for us?' And I said, 'Here am I. Send me!'"

In 2004, I was selected for the pinnacle warrant officer assignment of my career as the Personnel Proponent Warrant Officer at the Army Ordnance Center and School. My previous jobs, training, and combat experience had prepared me to become the eyes, ears, and brains of the Ordnance Corps. I was tasked with approving or disapproving applications for enlisted military personnel and civilians to become ordnance corps warrant officers. It was up to me to ensure that the program of instruction (POI) and curriculum for the 14 missile and electronic MOS positions in the Army at every ordnance school was relevant, rigorous, and reliable. This allowed me to drive the doctrine and training that would ripple through the Army for decades to come.

I traveled to all of the ordnance schools in the Army and reviewed all the POIs to secure proper funding for the curriculums, realign them with the new Army AirLand Battle vision, and prep the Ordnance Corps for its later transition to a modular force structure. That structure transitioned the Army from a traditional, division-based force into a brigade-based one so that different Army units would be matched with other units based on the skill sets and assets they possessed. I laid out all of the equipment, looked at every manual, and made sure each school had every resource it needed.

This work was my professional legacy, the thing I would be remembered for long after I retired, and I was lauded for my efforts that led to transforming and changing the methodology for training ordnance soldiers to support future Army transformation and modularity requirements. I was also part of the planning process for Army 2025, some of which was still playing out at the time this book was written. Finally, I was humbled to participate in the Army's think tank for the United States' response to weapons of mass destruction.

I did nothing by myself. I had great teams, and I tried to treat everyone the same whether they were a private or a general.

My Army career ended in August 2007 after I was diagnosed with prostate cancer in March of that year. I'll always remember looking at the magnetic resonance imaging (MRI) evidence and reading the report from the cancer center at John Hopkins University when I was diagnosed. I was alone when I was given the news. Erica was at another appointment that she couldn't miss. I told her that I would be fine, and that God had me, no matter what the results.

After seeing that I was positive for prostate cancer, I went back to my car and started crying before praying to God, through His Son, Jesus, to give me the strength to start my cancer journey with hope in my heart. I fired the ignition, and the first song that came on the radio was Tim McGraw's "Live Like You Are Dying." I smiled to myself and felt reassured to continue to live my life to the fullest.

Thankfully, my urologist was able to detect my cancerous cells early enough to allow me a chance to battle the same horrible disease that had taken Big Daddy's life in 1982. I asked the congregation at Bicentennial Chapel on Redstone Arsenal to please pray for me and my pending prostate surgery. I was ready for whatever fate God had set for me. Then a last pre-surgery examination declared the glorious miracle: the cancerous cells were gone! The truth of 1 Peter 2:24 resonated in my mind and heart. "'He himself bore our sins' in his body on the cross, so that we might die to sins and live for righteousness; 'by his wounds you have been healed.'" I felt like the leper in Luke 17, and I had to tell all those who had been praying for me just how great God was!

I was truly saddened that I had to end my career short of my 30-year service goal. I even went into a deep depression for a time, sensing that the job was not done. There were other things that I was in line to achieve—that I felt I deserved to achieve—but I was not going to be able to finish the way I wanted.

Yet I realized then, and recognize today, that I am still above ground. A lot of people I served with are not. My heart goes out to the families of the soldiers who did not come back from their service to the nation. I didn't fail myself or any of my soldiers. I gave the Army all that I had to give, and I didn't run away from any tough missions or assignments. I tried to always lead from the front and set the example for my troops whether in garrison or combat environments.

The Ordnance Corps Hall of Fame recognizes my entire body of work, and I dedicated it to the soldiers I served with. I hope the true legacy I left was the care that I had for my fellow soldiers, and that I had never asked them to do something that I wasn't willing to do myself.

During my military career, Erica and my family moved over 25 different times. We did it together. I wouldn't have wanted it any other way—and along the way, I experienced a lot about human nature and courage that have given me several lessons learned.

Allow me to now share those with you.

Chapter 9

THE FLAWED MAN'S PLAN
MEETS THE TRUTH

One of the rules I tried to live by during my Army career was to be my best at all times. I never knew who was watching me—plus my soldiers deserved my best since they were giving me their best, especially whenever we were in combat situations.

That being the case, the narrative of my life you just read teaches a vital overall truth that surpasses being your "best," and it is this: you must develop your character in peace time because it will come out in war time—in other words, develop it when things are going well because it will manifest itself in seasons of difficulty. If you are selfish, a liar, or tend to take the easy way out of conflict, that will be made clear during trials. If you are honest and a good leader, that will come out, too.

I've discovered the hard way that no one is perfect. You'll make mistakes along the way, and sometimes you'll make the same error more than once before you overcome it. As you now know, that's exactly what I did. My greatest failure was my poor parenting style and lack of patience with my children during their challenges in life. As I gave the military all of my effort, I shortchanged my family by not displaying the love, restraint, and forbearance they needed from me as a father and husband. You have to give the same or more attention and care to your family than you give to your work and others. How can you go to work and smile, but then not take care of your loved ones at home? Of course, that is exactly what the enemy of your soul, Satan, wants to happen so that you will feel guilty and hypocritical.

I didn't detail every hurdle I had with each of my children or with Erica—those are their stories to tell. But, at the end of the day, I can declare that it is only through the grace of God and His love that our most cherished relationships can be healed and restored.

Where are my children now? My son, who ended up spending over half his life locked away in a penitentiary for several felony-level offenses, is deceased. He had been released from prison for almost two years and was trying to live as a new Christian and a good citizen, but he continued to have somewhat of a prison mentality. As a result, he got into a heated argument with someone, and the person shot him at close range, ending his life. He was just 41. I didn't share how many times his mother, grandmother, and Erica and I tried to intervene and encourage him to get back on track, but God knows.

My oldest daughter became a family counselor after earning a master's degree in clinical mental health counseling and psychotherapy. She is now helping families, just like ours was when she was young, to learn how to communicate better and be a strong, loving, functional team. She and her husband have a daughter and a son.

My youngest daughter became a nurse and is currently serving as a medical officer in the Army reserves. As of this writing, she had begun her master's degree program, and has one daughter.

I thank God that my relationships with both of my daughters have healed, and we appreciate and love each other and do not hold old wounds against one another. We fly all our grandkids in several times a year to spend time together so we can have a strong bond. We build this bond by ensuring they get to visit one another and interact during summer trips and getaways as a family. It's wonderful, and Erica and I don't take a second of it for granted.

In the 15-plus years since I retired from the Army, I have mentored dozens of young people of both genders and several ethnicities. But I'll always wish that I would have done a better job trying to understand my own children. I thought I was making them tough so they could take on the world like I felt I had to do, but I only damaged the foundation of their lives instead of shoring it up. My children needed me to be kinder, gentler, and more understanding of their own individual journeys. They didn't need me barking orders at them and telling them all about my old war stories, be they from my Army experiences or my own upbringing.

The Bible tells us that charity, Godly love, starts at home. In 1 Timothy 5:8, it declares, "Anyone who does not provide for their relatives, and especially for their own household, has denied the faith and is worse than an unbeliever." Proverbs 13:24 adds, "Whoever spares the rod hates their children, but the one who loves their children is careful to discipline them."

I sought to provide for my family and caringly discipline my children, but I did both at the expense of driving those I loved to push back against my harsh tactics. I violated the exhortation in Ephesians 6:4 that says, "Fathers, do not exasperate your children; instead, bring them up in the training and instruction of the Lord." Time and again, Erica asked me to be kinder and gentler with our girls when they made mistakes. Yet I was so focused on my severely flawed "no mistake" mentality that I was too rigid and locked in to hear my wife's biblical voice of reason.

I wanted my children to be better than me and felt discipline and strictness was the way to boost them from poverty to success in one generation. I was wrong.

The Lord has forgiven me for my failures with my family, but Satan always tries to bring those flaws back up during my human moments of weaknesses and sadness—times when I think about "what could have been" for the loved ones I am separated from or have lost. By the grace of God, my grandchildren will never know the man, father, and husband that I used to be. I pray they will only know the man I am today—and how Jesus has transformed me into that better man as Romans 12:2 describes. "Do not conform to the pattern of this world, but be transformed by the renewing of your mind. Then you will be able to test and approve what God's will is—his good, pleasing and perfect will."

Although Christ saved me and fully redeemed me from my sins, there were many flaws in my life during my Army years that I had not yet addressed. I was transformed in Him, but I had not conformed to Him and His ways in several key areas. Today, I have corrected many of those shortcomings, and I am still working on others. Truth is, I will be until the day I die. Likewise, there were consequences from my poor choices that I had to endure, and there still may be consequences to come resulting from my past flaws.

But those outcomes do not define who I am now—and your flaws do not define who you are, either. As you give those to God and earnestly begin conforming yourself to His will for your life, you may make the same *four essential discoveries* that I made, too. My first discovery was that **all you truly have in this world is yourself and those you love.** Your accomplishments, possessions, and other relationships—the things and people you assign value to—are well and good. But you, your family, and your close friends are all that really matters. You do not want to wait to work things out with them until the day you are attending a funeral with a lifetime of regret weighing on your heart and soul, when you can't do anything more but turn it over to God.

It is best to do something today while you still can. However, if your family member or close friend will not allow you to work out your differences, all you can do is take it to the Lord in prayer and allow Him to work in that person's heart.

I have come to understand as a man that the most important responsibilities I have are as a husband and a father. I liken what we are given to take care of in life to being rubber balls and glass balls. If it is important, it is a glass ball. You can never drop it or else it will break. If it is not that important, it is a rubber ball. You can drop it, let it bounce and roll for a while, and pick it up later when all of the glass balls are secure and safe.

You, your family, your close friends, and your faith are glass balls.

What you do for a living, the items you have, and the other people in your life are rubber balls.

I wish I had figured that out earlier in life. Now that I have, I've also learned that having patience and tolerance with your close friends and family members so they have the chance to make their own decisions in life is an investment into their future that can unleash their destiny. I draw power and inspiration from Isaiah 41:10 ("Do not fear, for I am with you; do not be dismayed, for I am your God. I will strengthen you and help you; I will uphold you with my righteous right hand.") and Philippians 4:13 ("I can do all things through him who gives me strength.") to develop this patience and tolerance as I get older.

My next essential discovery was that **it takes a village to be successful in life.** It certainly did for me. I never imagined that a young biracial boy who was born out of wedlock and into poverty in the deep south in the middle of the color line could one day be inducted into two different Army Halls of Fame: the aforementioned Ordnance Corps Hall of Fame and The Eagle Rising Society Warrant Officer Hall of Fame. I joined the Army after high school because I knew the military would let me continue to grow as a person and reward me based on my hard work and efforts in ways similar to my Boy Scout experiences. I could tell early in my Army career that it provided a lifestyle where I could serve my country and make an honorable living. My mentors tell me that if we do well at the small things, big things will come our way. They're right!

I am grateful for all the leaders who tolerated me as I made mistakes early in my military career and allowed me to recover from those mistakes and be successful. If leaders today could just remember that they were once young and made errors, they might be less harsh and become more careful when making judgments that affect others. I was quite the work in progress throughout my Army years, and I thank God I had leaders who were patient enough to allow me to work through my shortcomings and character flaws, particularly when it came to integrity and telling the truth. It is ironic, after my Army career, that major organizations in north Alabama have given me opportunities for leadership that included being their truth teller.

I was able to utilize the leadership traits I gained in the Army to become a Junior Reserve Officers Training Corps (JROTC) instructor in the Huntsville City Schools. My youngest daughter was one of my JROTC students for one semester. When she was chosen to be cadet commander by her fellow students, it was a proud moment for me as her father, and I later had the joy of commissioning her as an officer in the Army after she graduated from her university's ROTC program.

I also started my own Limited Liability Company and became a consultant in the discipline of organization design and theory for the Huntsville and Madison, Alabama Police Departments, which led to me being selected as a spokesperson for the Huntsville police. I was often featured on the local news discussing crime and informing citizens how they could prevent becoming victims of crime. It wasn't without its dangers. As spokesperson, I was once digitally stalked by a citizen who was diagnosed with a mental illness, and I was also marked (a gang member pointed at me with his fingers extended like a gun) at a stop light. There is sometimes a price that comes with the notoriety and acknowledgement of a high visibility position. But there were incredible positives as well. During that time with the Huntsville police, Erica and I built an annual community program to help thousands of youths in north Alabama receive free school supplies, book bags, food, and networking information to help them become more successful. The Community Awareness For Youth hosted the largest youth event of its kind under our direction.

> I thank God I had leaders who were patient enough to allow me to work through my shortcomings and character flaws.

I was later hired as the community affairs spokesperson for Huntsville Utilities. I stayed there for three years prior to accepting a position as the site director and dean for the Florida Institute of Technology's Huntsville site, where I served for over a year. Next, I was asked to interview for a new position as vice president of employee engagement at Huntsville Utilities, and after an arduous interview process, I was hired as the first vice president of color in that company's history—the position I held as this book was completed.

For nearly two decades I have been one of the primary leaders for the Redstone Arsenal Army Christian Men's Group. I also help coach and manage the Redstone Arsenal 13-time defending champion Ten-Miler team. In addition, Erica and I conduct pre-marital counseling for young couples and lead young adult Bible studies in our community. Our goal is to share the lessons we've learned and to help others avoid the pitfalls we experienced as a Christian couple raising a family in this challenging world. Occasionally, I officiate the marriages of some of our young adults.

I have never forgotten those who have opened doors for me. It is hard to get to the next level in any organization or endeavor without someone on that level sponsoring you or giving you the opportunity to advance. One of my primary sponsors was a retired Army colonel I met in Germany in 1984. Little did I know then how our relationship would continue to grow and how his influence would open doors for me for almost 40 years. Be attentive and always treat others as if you are building a relationship with them for life.

My third essential discovery was to realize that **people are people, so it takes kindness to work with them.** I had to take some tough actions with co-workers and supervisors over the years, including reporting one senior leader for fraternization with a subordinate and another co-worker for racism and sexual harassment. I have acted as a human resources agent for organizations to terminate employees for cheating on their time-cards, stealing company property, bullying fellow employees, and failing drug and alcohol tests. I have been set up, slandered, sabotaged, and investigated based on false accusations, but each time the truth surfaced during the investigation, and I have been exonerated.

These are the experiences you may have when you're a leader charged with upholding high moral standards and unwilling to comply through your silence with those who are breaking standards of conduct. Yet as you embrace these realities and respond with kindness, even when you are not being treated kindly yourself, you will uphold your own integrity, protect your employer, and create other relationships that are based on kindness and respect. It won't be easy, but it will be more than worth the effort.

That leads to my last essential discovery, which is to **coexist with others with respect for one another.** In my role at Huntsville Utilities, I have been able to implement all of my lessons learned to help employees uniquely develop into the type of leaders who can grow and overcome their mistakes as they accept the consequences of their actions and decide to do better going forward. Those are the kind of people who give respect and are respected.

At Huntsville Utilities, I also guide co-workers into the best workspace experience obtainable, so each employee can lead the company in pursuit of a diverse and inclusive workforce. I have also been humbled since 2008 to teach at the Huntsville Police Academy on the topics of cultural awareness, ethics, and leadership principles. My prayer is that the training will allow people in our community to work with police officers who are more aware and respectful of cultural differences, resulting in a more peaceful community for everyone to live and thrive in.

In the course of all of these roles since my retirement from the Army, I have matured to a place where I no longer have that longtime military mindset to be the best.

I prefer to be a mentor or coach; I don't need to be your policeman.

I prefer to be your partner; I don't want to be your sheriff.

I prefer to be your shepherd; I don't want to be your boss.

I prefer to be your brother/co-worker/teammate.

The transformation in my leadership style has been nothing short of miraculous, and I thank God for the journey with all of its ups and downs, wins and losses, and triumphs and failures.

You will meet some people in life who soon become like family members, usually through your shared experiences and perhaps because you are both missing some key family relationships due to estrangement or death. You have no choice about the family you are born into, but you can sometimes pick those who will be like family to you.

I am fortunate to have two great people who have been like parents to Erica and me. Our stand-in mother is a strong, tough German lady we met in church. It was right after Erica's mom had passed away, the last of our biological parents to do so, that the lady told us she would be our mom. It was the sweetest thing, and Erica felt like crying. The lady could tell I was a little broken then, and she reached out to me in a motherly way that I wasn't expecting. Her husband, a retired U.S. military officer, is our stand-in father. Both have given advice and encouragement with honesty and conviction. They check in on us when we get sick or have challenges in life, just as parents would. It's been wonderful.

Erica and I also have what we call a "bonus" daughter, son, and grandson. The daughter was our youngest daughter's roommate from college, and we love her dearly. She is a Christian young lady with strong beliefs and morals who got involved in our family in such a way that we were easily able to adopt her as our own. The son is a young man who sought me out in 2018. He realized I was the first person of color in a lot of positions in Huntsville, and he asked me to become his mentor. We just went from there, developing a deep father-son bond from that relationship. The grandson, our youngest daughter's stepson, has been in our lives from an early age. We spoiled him (and still do) like only grandparents can.

We love all five of these additions to our existing families because we know God allowed them to intertwine with our lives and to lovingly grow close to us in a way that can only be described as family.

My modus operandi has always been to be polite, professional, positive, and passionate, four golden nuggets I have adopted from the leaders who have invested their time and wisdom in me. My goal in the workplace as a Christian is to try to be the best version of myself at all times and not be afraid of the four-letter word w-o-r-k. Good, old-fashioned work, along with earning the respect of others, are the keys to success.

> You can pursue your dreams with *purpose.*

You can obtain most of your life's goals if you stay *polite, professional, positive,* and *passionate.* You can also pursue your dreams with *purpose.*

Lastly, here are **eight final truths** that have helped me become a better leader and person. I am confident they will do the same for you.

1. **God is real as proven in the Holy Bible, through nature, and in your heart.**

   I believe you are born into this world with a desire to serve someone or something. The biggest decision you will make in life is deciding what that will be. There have been many times that God has directly intervened in my life that can only be described as supernatural. I do not know how anyone can read the Bible and not be touched in a personal way that only the truth can cause. I do not know how anyone can look at the glory and diversity of nature and not believe there is a grand designer behind it all who has put this world, and reality as we know it, into motion. Seek God, and you will find Him (Matthew 7:7).

2. **Rising above your circumstances will take help from God's agents on earth: other human beings.**

   My story is filled with people who helped me and opened the doors of success for me. I have received assistance and mentorship from a myriad of people and sponsors from across the globe who have shared their perspectives and life lessons, allowing me to learn from their victories and failures. Remember what you believe and where you came from (2 Peter 1:12). Appreciate how much help and sponsorship you have received to get to where you are today—then pass it on. Always pay it forward!

3. **Being persistent and consistent over time can make up for your lack of privilege or opportunities.**

It's an undeniable truth in our society that others in privileged positions succeed over less fortunate people. However, I realized early that the only way I could make up for my lack of privilege as a young person was to work harder and smarter than my peers. God gave me an engine that has boundless energy, and I focused it in three areas. I kept physically fit. I read books, inspired by how Benjamin Franklin had decided to read as many books as possible to broaden his mind. I set goals. I've had a binder now for 40 years where I write and track all of my goals, and I've accomplished most of them. I once showed it to my daughters so they could see how I wrote down all the small steps it takes to achieve goals. It isn't magic. It's a marathon, and I had to move toward the completion of my goals each day.

By working harder and more efficiently, I believe I show myself as a worker who is approved by God (2 Timothy 2:15). If you feel you are beset by a lack of privilege or opportunities, please pray and ask God to allow the talents He has blessed you with to be increased and amplified so you can become the best version of yourself to succeed and help others do the same. Ephesians 1:3 declares, "Praise be to the God and Father of our Lord Jesus Christ, who has blessed us in the heavenly realms with every spiritual blessing in Christ." The Lord has given you the tools, but it is up to you to persistently and consistently utilize them to benefit yourself, you family, and your community.

4. **Faith, family and friends, finances, and fitness must be managed to be wholly successful in life.**

Each one of these four F's are vital. *Faith* comes from discovering the truth in the Bible and then taking on those truths as the basis for your personal beliefs (Romans 10:17). You can manage your faith to be successful by starting each day with Bible study or a devotional message. Most every morning, Erica reads a daily devotion aloud, so we begin the day focused and filled with the knowledge of Jesus Christ. Starting your day similarly will allow you to be ready for the challenges that lie ahead.

Family is built through the relationships you form and nurture with *family* members and close *friends* (1 Timothy 3:4). These relationships are managed as you work out your differences and live through the ups and downs of life together. The key is forgiveness. Colossians 3:13 encourages you to "bear with each other and forgive one another if any of you has a grievance against someone. Forgive as the Lord forgave you." Forgiveness is a choice. It is a decision of your will, motivated by obedience to God and His command to forgive. Forgiveness is a call to action that must be nurtured and practiced every day if you truly want to have peace in your life.

Finances cover the attitudes you have, and actions you take, regarding money and wealth. The Scriptures warn us in Deuteronomy 18:17-18, "You may say to yourself, 'My power and the strength of my hands have produced this wealth for me.' But remember the Lord your God, for it is he who gives you the ability to produce wealth, and so confirms his covenant, which he swore to your ancestors, as it is today." You will manage your finances best by ensuring you take care of those obligations that are like glass balls, paying them on time and in full, while meeting your other monetary responsibilities that are like rubber balls and let them bounce a while until the mandatory needs are met. Of course, this is enabled as you first give back to the Lord by financially supporting your local church and community with tithes, offerings, and donations (Malachi 3:8-10).

Fitness refers to how you take care of your body by eating well and exercising, knowing that your body is the physical temple God has given you (1 Corinthians 6:19-20). This is managed as you strive to maintain a healthy lifestyle and workout regimen. If you cannot do this because of some physical or logistical challenge, do what your body allows you to do as best as you can.

5. **Watch your words, especially when you are angry and feel as if you have lost all of your patience.**
Another undeniable truth is that your words will be remembered, and you will be held accountable for them. I have said many things that I regret, and I have experienced the consequences for those words. There are some people that I may be separated from for life unless God intervenes in their hearts to forgive me for what I said to them. What you speak can hurt and corrupt (James 3:6), so how do you watch your words when you are upset or impatient? Take a moment to breathe and pray for the correct words to say before you speak. Don't just declare what is on your mind at that moment. I have found that doing so often expresses a thought that came straight from Satan himself. Even if you believe you are right and the other person is wrong, you could say something that could damage that relationship,

possibly for good. Remember Proverbs 25:11. "Like apples of gold in settings of silver is a ruling rightly given."

6. **Prayer and God's Word are the most powerful weapons you will ever have to succeed in life.**

Prayer is so important. Why? It can bring peace, deliverance, and healing to yourself and those for whom you are praying—especially when they are seasoned and empowered by your knowledge and use of the Bible, identified in Ephesians 6:17 as the "sword of the Spirit" and as a "double-edged sword" in Hebrews 4:12. You develop these weapons in your life by knowing God, asking for His help, reading and studying the Word of God, and practicing what you learn from Him in your daily life. I have obtained two doctorate degrees and several certifications during my pursuit of education, but there is no higher level of learning than what the Bible has imparted to me. Only God our Father, through His Son Jesus Christ, and the empowerment and equipping of His Holy Spirit, can get you through this life and take you to your eternal rest in Heaven.

7. **Always take the hard right over the easy wrong.**

It took me a while to become a genuinely honest person, but God never gave up on me, and He continues to help me choose right over wrong, according to His Word (Proverbs 1:3). Yet when you decide to do what is right, God will close some doors and open others, for He knows what is best for you. You'll consistently make the hard right choices over the easy wrong ones as you rely on the principles and directives of the Word of God to instruct and guide you. As a flawed man with a history of making the easy wrong decisions at different junctures of my life, I know that you can change and transform who you are, a little bit at a time, day by day, as you obey the Lord.

8. **There is always a price to pay for success, so make sure the cost is not too high.**

I have dropped a few glass balls in my life that may never be repaired this side of Heaven. If the price for success means putting your family on the altar as if they are a sacrifice for your success, then I recommend you redefine your definition of success, starting with 1 Timothy 5:8. It says, "Anyone who does not provide for their relatives, and especially for their own household, has denied the faith and is worse than an unbeliever." True success begins and ends at home.

You wish to succeed. The heart of the American Dream is to be successful financially and educationally, and I have achieved that dream according to its narrow definition. But if I could do it all over again, I would be softer, kinder, and more understanding of my family's needs as I chased my American Dream. I would have done a better job balancing my ambition and drive to the top with being more sensitive to my family. I can only thank God that I have a Christian wife and forgiving children who have accompanied me through my journey. *They* are the only success that truly matters.

> I know that you can change and transform who you are, a little bit at a time.

In closing, I would implore anyone to always tell the truth, even when the truth is not convenient, because in the final ledger of life, the truth always wins, and it will set you free (John 8:32).

For Erica and I, telling our full story has been freeing and cathartic. However, we know there will be a price to pay for sharing our truth with the world. It's inevitable someone from our story may get offended at what we've revealed, but all I can say is that God gave us permission to share our story as it is written. Erica received that very message from the Lord in her heart first, and I pushed back against it for several months because of my foolish pride and wanting my reputation to stay untainted. But I finally realized that God was also confirming in my heart that I needed to be willing to tell our story so that others who have been, or may still be, on a similar road can know the truth and have the opportunity to apply it to their lives.

I had to let the truth fall where it may.

If this book helps just one person forgive themselves, forgive others, show more kindness, or make one less mistake, then it is worth the time and effort it took to write it.

Psalm 32 says this.

Blessed is the one whose transgressions are forgiven, whose sins are covered.

Blessed is the one whose sin the Lord does not count against them and in whose spirit is no deceit.

When I kept silent, my bones wasted away through my groaning all day long.

For day and night your hand was heavy on me; my strength was sapped as in the heat of summer.

Then I acknowledged my sin to you and did not cover up my iniquity. I said, "I will confess my transgressions to the Lord." And you forgave the guilt of my sin.

Therefore let all the faithful pray to you while you may be found; surely the rising of the mighty waters will not reach them.

You are my hiding place; you will protect me from trouble and surround me with songs of deliverance.

I will instruct you and teach you in the way you should go; I will counsel you with my loving eye on you.

Do not be like the horse or the mule, which have no understanding but must be controlled by bit and bridle or they will not come to you.

Many are the woes of the wicked, but the Lord's unfailing love surrounds the one who trusts in him.

Rejoice in the Lord and be glad, you righteous; sing, all you who are upright in heart!

Writer and theologian, Thomas Merton, is credited with saying, "Pride makes us artificial. Humility makes us real." Devotional author, Boyd Bailey, founder of Wisdom Hunters, Inc., once wrote, "Humble people leave behind a residue of God, not themselves."

The bottom line is this: Pride makes us artificial, fake, and superfluous. But humility, empowered by forgiveness, makes us real. It makes us transparent.

It makes us genuine.

Just like Erica and I, you want to leave a legacy in this life— but you must not get confused and think the legacy is for you. It isn't. Your legacy must be to leave that residue of Jesus in people's lives so that even if they forget about you (and they almost certainly will), they will remember *Him*. The focus should always be on Jesus.

Philippians 2:3-4 teaches, "Do nothing out of selfish ambition or vain conceit. Rather, in humility value others above yourselves, not looking to your own interests but each of you to the interests of the others." God has given you abilities, talents, and a mind to think well. So, whatever it is you achieve in life, and however many flaws of your own you have to face and overcome in the process—it is *all* to His glory.

It's not about you.

It's about Him.

I never thought I would write a tell-all book about my life, but I have. I want you to know that God is real—and the only way I could express that was by sharing my life in all of its victories and failures to emphasize how great and forgiving God is. Erica and I are still working on ourselves and our relationships with our family. We know God is still working on us because we are both flawed—and that is why we continue to put our plans in God's hands!

Christ declares in John 14:6, "I am the way and the truth and the life. No one comes to the Father except through me." Joshua 24:15 declares, "But if serving the Lord seems undesirable to you, then choose for yourselves this day whom you will serve, whether the gods your ancestors served beyond the Euphrates, or the gods of the Amorites, in whose land you are living. But as for me and my household, we will serve the Lord."

I hope this book inspires you to allow Jesus into your life. It is only through Him that you can live a better, fuller life with fewer flaws and more joy!

www.ingramcontent.com/pod-product-compliance
Lightning Source LLC
Chambersburg PA
CBHW060908120626
46553CB00001B/250